PFA

PROTO-TYPING FOR ARCHI-TECTS

Mark Burry & Jane Burry

With more than 700 illustrations

 Thames & Hudson

First published in the United Kingdom
in 2016 by Thames & Hudson Ltd,
181A High Holborn, London WC1V 7QX

First paperback edition 2017

Prototyping for Architects © 2016
Thames & Hudson Ltd, London

Foreword © 2016 Bob Sheil

Text © 2016 Mark Burry and Jane Burry

Photographs © 2016 the copyright
holders; see page 271

British Library Cataloguing-in-
Publication Data

A catalogue record for this book
is available from the British Library

ISBN 978-0-500-29249-5

Printed and bound in China by Everbest
Printing Co. Ltd

To find out about all our publications,
please visit **www.thamesandhudson.com**.
There you can subscribe to our
e-newsletter, browse or download our
current catalogue, and buy any titles
that are in print.

Front cover, top image.
3XN, 'Learning from Nature' pavilion,
Louisiana Museum of Modern Art,
Humlebæk, Denmark, 2009
(see page 189)

Front cover, bottom image.
ICD, ICD/ITKE Research Pavilion,
University of Stuttgart, Germany,
2012 (see page 219)

Back cover, top image.
Rory Hyde, 'Bin Dome', *Melbourne
Now*, National Gallery of Victoria,
Melbourne, Australia, 2013–14
(see page 60)

Back cover, bottom image.
OCEAN Design Research Association,
Flying Compression canopy, Nusfjord,
Lofoten, Norway, 2013
(see page 259)

Contents

3

4

5

Foreword

Bob Sheil

Dependency between the drawn and the made is a bond that allows either realm something unique to explore and something plural to create. The world between also includes all the writing, images, models, conversations, keepsakes and behaviours that contribute to the ancient and intuitive human activity surrounding the act of building. In this regard, both the prototype and prototyping are loaded with content, meaning, potential and mystique, somewhere between part-architecture and architecture-plus. With their oscillating rawness and polished finesse, their positive naivety and outrageous ambition, they signal where architecture and the large number of players involved in its production can, could or should go. When this is understood imaginatively and intelligently, both product and process become laden with rich and vast pickings that permeate the repertoire of an industry permanently at risk of playing things safe.

So the first thing a prototype has to be is an enterprise that takes risks – one of which is to challenge the premise on which it was commissioned, another to challenge all those involved to see how the part they need to (or indeed could) play in the game should change. Prototypes that simply reaffirm an assertion have a role, of course, but those that provoke a significant rethink are considerably more powerful. Having the confidence to reject an outcome is perhaps the primary and most important duty of the designer, who must recognize that there is a fundamental difference between what they made through drawing and what the drawing made, and how there is a world of difference in-between.

A prototype is both a question and an answer. An agent provocateur. A dry run. A rehearsal. A preview. And, at its best, a revelation. The prototype is architecture of neither here nor there, a projective and a reflective act, somewhere between a castaway and a hidden treasure.

Taking prototypes literally might provide useful data, but to do so alone can miss the entire point. Prototypes and prototyping in design are not scientific or technical exercises; neither are they mere demonstrators, or simulations of the real. Rather, they are layered entities, acts of theatre and performance that examine the translation of the abstract into the tactile where all members of the audience, possessing a copy of the performance programme so to speak, leave the show with a different and valid interpretation of what they witnessed. Prototypes, in other words, enable us to overcome the barriers of representation and fabrication, allowing messier forms of human and environmental context to wield their dirty influence – for instance, how scale and meaning operate differently between the place of design, the place of production, and the place of rest.

This welcome and spectacular book has been exquisitely collated with many of the motivations and readings mentioned above. It is wide-ranging, curious, diverse and provocative. It allows the reader to accept or discard the propositions each researcher has made to inform the dilemmas and opportunities available in architecture today. It captures the way in which prototypes and prototyping have been accelerated by progressive technologies and methods in representation and fabrication, and, with this, exciting new domains in which the designer and the maker can reside, collaborate and morph. Despite the popular and misguided scepticism that lingers over the construction and design industries, it powerfully illustrates how these sibling agencies are populated with abundant creative capital, immense devotion and inspiring expertise.

Professor Bob Sheil, Director of the Bartlett School of Architecture

Introduction

What is prototyping for architects?
Who is this book for?
How has the book been organized?
The terrain surveyed, but for what purpose?
How has the review of current practice been presented?
What gaps is the book intended to fill?

1–2

1–4. Students at work, Ulm School of Design (Hochschule für Gestaltung Ulm), Ulm, Germany, 1953–68. The Ulm School's innovative approach to design was implemented through the departments of Product Design, Visual Communication, Industrialized Building, Information and Film-making.

What is prototyping for architects?

Prototyping for architects looks at every aspect of the realization of ideas, experiments and investigations as physical or digital artefacts during the design process. Prototyping itself is more than the representational and abstract intentions behind modelling, because included in the activity is an element of novelty and testing. A model of a steam engine as a historical record, for example, is not the same as James Watt's first working scale prototype of his groundbreaking invention. Designers prototype their designs in order to test them. Whether the prototype actually works is not the issue: prototyping is the revelatory process through which a designer gains insight into how well their experiment is proceeding. Failure offers important information, which, when fed back into the creative process, increases the chances of a more successful outcome. Prototyping is therefore an essential part of every designer's repertoire. Why, then, a book on prototyping for architects if prototyping is already such an important aspect of the architectural design process?

Three recent developments have helped bring this book into being. First, we live in an age in which the incursion into the design process of new miniaturized technologies has led to an expectation of far quicker turnaround times. Rapid prototyping, which almost always implies the use of miniaturized technologies, has resulted in clients expecting to be shown a series of prototypes in quick succession. Secondly, the miniaturization of rapid prototyping has in itself helped to create an environment in which the specialist model-maker is no longer the only person able to provide believable models of a given design. This has enabled the designer to be far more involved in prototyping than before. As a consequence, more prototyping can occur along the way – and in far greater detail – than was previously the case, and the design process itself is usefully distorted. In other words, the practice of the designer is evolving along with the changes in prototyping opportunities. Thirdly, new technologies continue to emerge, whether additive (3D printing, for example) or subtractive (such as robot milling), and are leading to quite unexpected consequences in terms of what we can and cannot do within our respective disciplines. Although we have been lured into protectionist practice through membership of the professional groups spawned by the medieval guilds – think of the operatives in ink-stained brown coats maintaining the printing presses, the metalworkers in grey coats oiling their lathes, the plaster technicians making models in their white jackets – the highly specific modes of design exploration of each of these groups have largely disappeared. Who, even as little as two decades ago, would have imagined the gathering of 2D designers, 3D designers and design engineers around the same equipment to produce a series of prototypes? This convergence not only offers considerable enrichment to each design discipline but also blurs the boundaries between the disciplines in ways that have the potential to be highly creative. It is this disruption in particular, together with the increasing speed of the design process and the empowerment of the amateur prototype-maker, that has inspired the writing of this book.

Who is this book for?

Prototyping for Architects is aimed at every architect (and 3D designer) at every stage of their career, from student to accomplished professional. To the student, a whole world of opportunity will be revealed. To the seasoned architectural practitioner, especially those who have been strongly discipline-based, the book

3–4

reflective practice carried out by the individual designer as they develop their proposals through prototyping.

Part 2 is a survey of the different kinds of prototyping available to the designer. The various modes of prototype production, from traditional and current practice to the most esoteric and evolving prototyping technologies, are explored and summarized systematically. The question of 'what does this mean for the relatively poorly resourced design student compared with the well-financed professional?' is dealt with implicitly at every step of the way. In addition, a look at how to access the technology conventionally is complemented by an examination of a selection of more unorthodox approaches, emphasizing that the designer does not necessarily give up their creative instincts when involving the latest technology.

The hint of the subversive in Part 2 drives the content of Part 3, a series of case studies of some of the leading designers currently at work in the fields of architecture and other, closely related areas of 3D design. In each case, a highly conspicuous and renowned practitioner has been examined through their practice. A combination of independent scholarship, conversation and observation is used to study their approach to prototyping, the aim being to stimulate the reader into new ways of thinking about their own approach to design and its development.

Finally, Part 4 offers a conclusion to the book by considering the role of prototyping through the ages, while Part 5 is intended to provide the reader with some additional resources, including a glossary of the key terms used in prototyping and a list of websites of the featured practices.

The book has been produced in large format to allow for the inclusion of a wide range of illustrations, such as professional, high-quality photographs of buildings at various stages of construction, building details, and models and prototypes of exemplar projects. Sketches and working drawings from the designers themselves have been included at their suggestion.

offers inviting glimpses of alternative modes of practice, coaxing them into new ways of working and experimenting. In this context, the book's main focus is the root activity of 'design speculation', espousing and developing it through a wide-ranging examination of prototyping in the twenty-first century. The book is intended not only to stimulate architects' creative instincts, but also to play its part in blurring the boundaries between the disciplines, which, driven by other instincts, have been unhelpfully protectionist in the past.

How has the book been organized?

The book is divided into five parts. Part 1 provides an introduction to the topic of prototyping in architecture. In a detailed yet accessible way, it examines the entire design-practice landscape, describes the various design disciplines to which architecture relates, and explores the differences in approach between these disciplines. Furthermore, it introduces the reader to the differences between design as a formal, declarative act seeking to inform third parties, and the highly personal act of

The terrain surveyed, but for what purpose?

There is nothing like fieldwork to provide a balance between theory and practice. Once we had begun our conversations with our chosen architectural and design firms – those in which prototyping plays an important role, at whatever stage of the design process – we became aware of a greater distinction between the different approaches taken. It became clear that, for the purposes of the book, detaching theory from practice would be less rewarding than the

5–6

5. ULM School of Design: Students at work.

6. Buckminster Fuller (1895–1983), the American architect, systems theorist and inventor, pictured with models of the lattice shell structures – or geodesic domes – for which he became famous.

thoughts on the difference between mock-ups and prototypes, discovering that the distinction was far clearer for some than for others.

For readers anticipating a clear set of definitions, the following extracts from the *Oxford English Dictionary* are little more than placeholders:

Prototype The first or primary type of anything; the original (thing or person) of which another is a copy, imitation, representation, or derivative, or to which it conforms or is required to conform; a pattern, model, standard, exemplar, archetype.

Model A representation in three dimensions of some projected or existing structure, or of some material object artificial or natural, showing the proportions and arrangement of its component parts.

Mock-up An experimental model (often full-sized) of a projected aircraft, ship, apparatus, etc., used esp. for study, testing, practice, or display.

On looking at Part 3 of this book, the section covering the nine prototyping taxonomies that emerged as a result of our conversations with fifty practices, the reader will soon discover that the world of practice plays quite fast and loose with these terms.

We were also interested in learning whether scale played a part, and in how close a facsimile the prototype needed to be when compared with the final design. Answers varied here too, with some practices regarding a prototype as something that 'worked', a testing base for whatever was being elicited from what was effectively design experimentation; in other cases, the prototype's appearance needed to be as close to the final design as possible. In such circumstances the prototype could almost be fulfilling the same role as a mock-up. In the case of the experimental prototype, however, neither scale nor faithful verisimilitude had any hard and fast design importance, given the prototype's testing purposes.

Digital prototyping is a relatively new technology, offering designers the opportunity to bypass to some degree the physical side of experimentation and testing, but attitudes to making what is essentially a leap of faith vary considerably. At the more traditional end of the spectrum, practitioners look perplexed: why on earth would we dabble in that dark art when we have everything we need already, including increasing access to sophisticated rapid-prototyping equipment? It seems to come down to what each designer wants to simulate and

alternative approach of educating the reader through a loosely structured exposé of the extraordinary variety of what we were finding in the field. What follows is a distillation of the route by which we were able to extract information from practices that vary greatly in size, financial circumstances, experience and their approach to new technology. Pre-eminent practices were selected on the basis that their work suggested rich terrain.

The first question we asked was simply, 'What is a prototype?' In almost every one of the fifty practices we visited, there was a long pause – sometimes a very long pause – before a response was offered. Although we never received the same answer twice, a taxonomy of sorts gradually emerged. Outlined later in the introduction, this taxonomy was used to structure the major part of this book.

Once we had established a view of what 'prototyping for architects' meant for each of our chosen practices, we went on to explore the difference between models and prototypes, whether there was a clear distinction between the two, and whether the practice deployed both. Similarly, we probed those we spoke to for their

7–8

they employ it regardless of whether the client is paying for it or not. Enlightened clients working with practices known for their prototyping-based approach to design – an approach usually well signposted by the practice – are happy to see the relevant costs built into the fees they are charged. Those practices that are happy to absorb the prototyping costs within a general fee basis argue that they do so because it is not always possible to anticipate the need to prototype when agreeing the fees for a particular job. However, they also recognize that prototyping can avoid expensive design 'blind alleys' by highlighting unexpected opportunities as well as certain risks, ultimately benefiting the practice as much as any other party.

When it comes to contractors building prototypes of their own volition, it is fair to say that this is generally more the exception than the rule: if prototyping is to be included as part of the building process, then the costs need to be included in the builders' tenders. Some practices note, however, that in certain situations building contractors have produced prototypes in order to find the most cost-effective and thus profitable route to achieving the architect's complex propositions.

The question of who pays for prototyping when it is carried out during the design process seems like a grey area only when the practice is shoehorned into a conventional, competitively tendered post-design contract. Because contemporary buildings intended to make a major public statement, whether they be a railway station or a national museum, tend towards greater spatial and constructional complexity, prototyping in these cases can clearly make a significant contribution – towards resolving design issues, meeting the architects' aspirations, securing building contractors' confidence with regard to achievable construction, and maintaining clients' confidence that what they have paid for will be delivered without financial surprises.

Our survey of prototyping in architecture concluded on a more pragmatic note, with questions intended to find out exactly what prototypes are being used to test, whether it be joints, complex geometry, weathering, acoustics, heat transfer, lighting performance or structure. Each of these areas can be the subject of fundamental investigations, depending on the context and, in some cases, the need to conform to a practice's 'signature' style. The differences between an architectural prototype and an industrial prototype were also probed, with responses ranging from definite positions at either end of the spectrum to something more ambivalent in between. Generally speaking,

who their audience might be. Beyond looking slightly perplexed at the suggestion that digital prototyping has a place, as opposed to merely representing a design in digital form, actual hostility to the concept can be encountered: an impossibility for some to accommodate the idea that a designer might abrogate their responsibilities to investigate a design through time-honoured manual endeavour. On the other hand, those in practice who fully embrace digital prototyping attest to the opportunities it offers to take architectural practice down entirely new avenues, some of which are explored later in this book. Opinions on digital prototyping vary across the profession, with some saying that digital prototyping might actually replace the physical kind, and others that digital and traditionally procured prototyping are different things for different purposes.

Another area of enquiry was whether practices have seen any changes in their clients' attitudes towards the practice of producing prototypes. That is, who pays for the prototype? Is it something that clients typically pay for?

For many practices, prototyping is such an important part of the design process that

7. Jean Prouvé (1901–1984), prefabricated petrol station, 1953, installed at Vitra Design Museum, Weil am Rhein, Germany, 2003.

8. The German architect and structural engineer Frei Otto (1925–2015) in his studio, 7 June 2004. Frei was noted for his development of especially lightweight structures.

9–10

9. Adjustable chair-design tool, Charles Eames (1907–1978) and Ray Eames (1912–1988), 1944: The Eames Office created this device within its first decade of operation. The intention behind the device was to gain a better understanding of the way people sit.

10. 'Kazam!' machine, Charles and Ray Eames, 1942: The Eameses' early experiments in making moulded-plywood chairs involved a laborious process of gluing and bonding thin layers of timber veneer. Key to this process was the 'Kazam!' machine, a device featuring hinged pieces of timber bolted together to withstand the high pressures necessary for forming the wood.

it would seem that design prototyping crosses disciplinary boundaries with little or no care for long-established professional niceties.

How has the review of current practice been presented?

The survey of prototyping practice within different architectural offices and cultures has been organized into a very loose taxonomy that groups together like approaches, attitudes to the prototype and philosophies of prototyping. The section headings draw on individual practitioners' own definitions of a prototype. For us, this produced more stimulating juxtapositions than a division strictly along the lines of technique or technology, or typological similarities among prototypes. Many of the practices could sit comfortably within several of our categories, and so we hope that the organization of the material will give to the reader the pleasure and excitement that we have enjoyed in talking to the many distinguished contributing designers, without the attribution of too much significance to our taxonomy.

Many of those we talked to referred to the prototype as a tool for underpinning their thinking and/or feeling during the design process. In this respect, a prototype could be a locale, an object for reflection, or a physical test with surprising feedback. In some cases, this might lead to an almost meditative interaction between designer and prototype. In others, the prototype is used to provide clarity when thinking about, and structuring, a design problem or proposition. The prototype as a tool for thinking/feeling is thus the topic of the first section of the survey.

A recurring observation among the practices we met with was that every architectural project is unique and hence prototypical in its entirety. Nevertheless, the serial prototyping opportunities, for a practice or design team, in working from one project to the next was also a topic of discussion. We have grouped those who emphasized this aspect of prototyping in the second section of the survey: the project as prototype.

Prototyping is, for many, a way to test – be it physically or, less often, digitally – whether or not a design proposition that has developed to a promising level actually works. To those we have grouped in the third section of the survey, architects and designers for whom prototyping is primarily an exercise in experimental verification or falsification, failure is a hugely important part of the design process, while partial success is equally useful in directing the creation of successive prototypes.

The fourth section, prototyping process for workflow, includes those practitioners engaged in the prototyping of processes or sequences and systems of design production in order to get them right. Areas of interest for such practitioners include actual craft-based construction and how to underpin it with information systems, as in the case of Archi-Union Architects; the prototyping of workflows incorporating underlying algorithms and the structuring of design and production processes using computer software, such as the work of Marble Fairbanks; and the building and testing of software prototypes, as carried out by Case Inc. All the practitioners in this section are deeply interested in systems.

The prototype, to quote Arup engineer Hugo Mulder, is the first thing you build. According to Michael Taylor at Hopkins Architects, it is a 'dry run'. Sometimes, it is even incorporated into the final work. In the fifth section of the survey, the practices spoken with address five different aspects of the prototype as a very concrete, albeit changeable, manifestation of what is to be built.

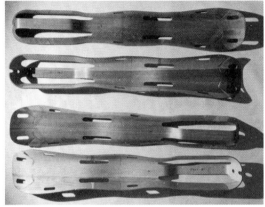

11–12

11. Aircraft fuselage, Charles and Ray Eames, 1943: In conjunction with the Molded Plywood Division of Evans Products, the Eameses constructed a variety of moulded-plywood parts for the fuselages of aircraft used by the US Navy. In addition to creating tail sections and gliders, they produced these so-called blisters, large sections of fuselage formed from a single piece of timber.

12. Leg splint, Charles and Ray Eames, 1943: The Eameses created these splints from timber veneer, which they bonded together with a resin glue and shaped into compound curves using a process involving heat and pressure. The slats between the timber allowed medical workers to pass cloth through the splint and secure the patient's leg.

The sixth section deals with the prototype as a site for the investigation and observation of behaviour under different conditions, whether it be the structural performance of an assembly, its water resistance, its response to other aspects of the environment, its material characteristics, or the responses of synthesized materials and diverse materials used in combination. This section, then, focuses on performance testing.

A prototype can be a manifestation or view of a primarily algorithmic or virtual system, or it can exist in a reciprocal relationship between the algorithm, with its rich possibilities, and the act of making. It can emerge from, and test, the experience of designed space, as well as being used to explore form and physical behaviour. The seventh section is a multifaceted investigation, through the voices of diverse, expert practitioners, of the prototype as a manifestation of data.

In the eighth section, the discourse takes a decidedly philosophical turn as the speakers explore the deeper meaning of the terms 'proto' and 'type'. In particular, they examine the significance of its role as a progenitor.

The ninth and final section of the survey explores prototyping's inherent ambivalence, whether it is process or product that is being addressed. In this section we gain some insight, through example, of the social, team-building and design paradigm-shaping roles in which the prototype can find itself.

What gaps is the book intended to fill?

This extensive survey of contemporary prototyping practice is based on a review of exemplar projects complemented by face-to-face conversations with fifty influential practitioners located on four continents. It is the first book to explore in depth a loose taxonomy of architectural prototyping processes aimed at gauging the likely success of a proposed innovation, whether it be in terms of design and/or functional performance. The book considers design expertise situated either within the field of architecture, or across related disciplines but contextualized through direct reference to specific architectural design projects.

Prototyping for Architects avoids being a coldly neutral survey. Wherever possible, we have incorporated historical and philosophical perspectives within an unashamed focus on contemporary 'how to' considerations and applications for architecture and related design practitioners.

Finally, this book examines radically new technologies and materials principally through examples drawn from practice. By considering a rich and diverse selection of these examples, we have been able to speculate on the future direction of prototyping within the spatial design disciplines that, as we understand it, constitute architecture today. Many of the singular approaches discovered during our research for this book are foregrounded in the following pages; perhaps, in the years ahead, such individual practice will eventually become mainstream professional endeavour.

Prototyping Techniques

Within architecture, prototyping has been brought into sharp relief by the enthusiastic adoption of such rapid CNC (computer numerical control) technologies as 3D printing, CNC routing and laser cutting. These technologies have made quick and repeated prototyping – testing iteratively, particularly within the design studio, at a reasonable cost – a reality. They have also made possible the rapid creation of disposable, bastardizable prototypes in such architecturally related industries as furniture design. There, they have displaced a very different animal: the painstakingly handcrafted prototype of the whole product, executed once, or at most twice as a proof of concept, with the artistic diligence of many days' work.

The use of such prototyping technologies has divided opinion. On the one hand, there is a residual disquiet about the way in which rapid CNC prototyping from digital models, used casually, creates an illusion of making in which none of the really critical issues, in terms of detailing and assembly, are ever encountered. In this scenario, there is none of the intimate interaction with the object or assembly experienced by the handworker, and no real understanding of the built artefact or architecture acquired through the process of prototype-making. There is, it is felt, a potential cognitive deficit – a contradiction of the basic premise of prototyping as an aid to thought. The use of 3D printing in particular can result in a homogenous outcome in which the fertile interactions between components, materials and different design considerations and criteria are obscured and lose their potency.

On the other hand, say its defenders, CNC-based prototyping often only partially automates production from digitally generated models and templates, leaving all the lessons of assembly to be discovered through human agency, especially at the architectural scale.

Moreover, the CNC processes themselves are so rich in parameters, many of which are not always within the control of the designer or designer-programmer, that unexpected variation still occurs – differences in dimensions or detailing produced by different laser-cutting machines or routers, for instance, that alert the designer to the production parameters, possibilities and tolerances. Digital prototyping has proved its mettle as a fast, affordable way to create subtle variants of a single digital model or script: phenotypes from a genetic archetype.

In this section we begin by briefly revisiting some traditional, often ingenious techniques for constructing prototypes. This provides us with both a useful baseline and a basis for the comparison of prototyping in architecture with its use in other areas of design. We then examine the different kinds of mock-up, including the high-fidelity variety, intended to emulate all the qualities of the final, built design. Next we focus on techniques for prototyping performance – in other words, the use of prototyping to measure and analyse how a design performs according to various criteria, such as structurally, thermally, in relation to light falling on it or passing through it, acoustically, and in terms of the user's experience. How, we ask, do these aspects of prototyping feed back into the design process? We then explore in more detail the impact of CNC technologies in architectural prototyping; subtractive technologies, such as milling, routing and laser cutting; and additive technologies, including printing and deposition. These, more task-specific technologies are then contrasted with the versatility and complexity offered by the adoption of robotics. Finally, we examine virtual prototyping – as more than a mere proposition – and provide the groundwork for asking whether there is indeed such a thing as a digital prototype.

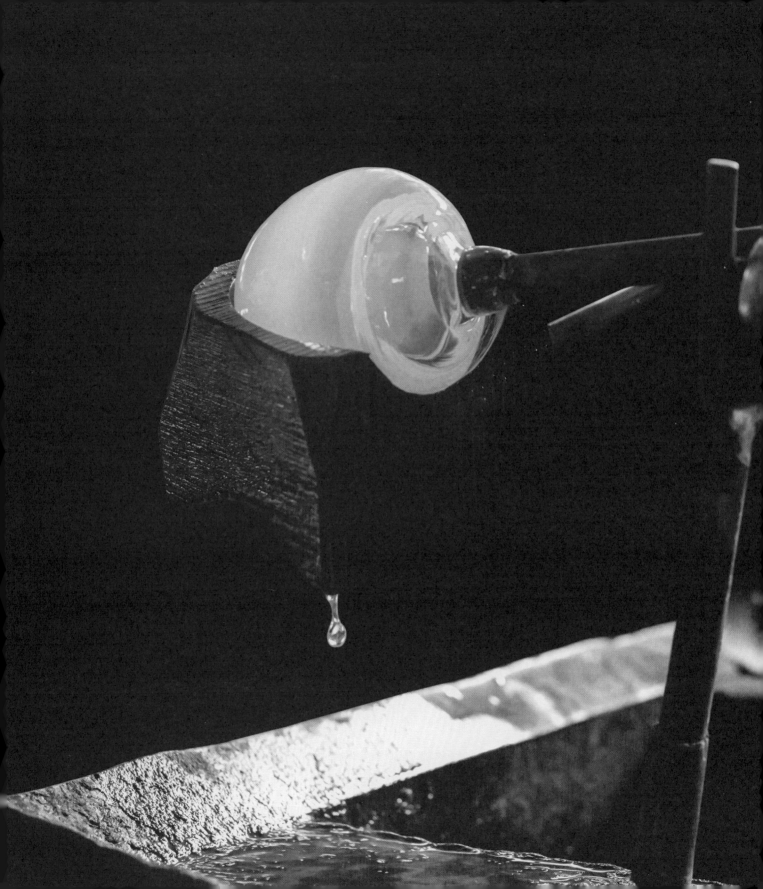

2.1

In Practice →
3.25 / p. 98 / Thomas Heatherwick
3.53 / p. 170 / Studio Gang
3.82 / p. 234 / BKK Architects

Traditional Techniques

A traditional prototyping technique is any technique that predates the introduction of the computer – or, more specifically, the computer numerical control (CNC) device – into the design studio. At their most basic, traditional techniques include the making of prototypes using such simple, handheld tools as the hammer and saw, implements that have been around for millennia and can be found in many different cultures. Following the Industrial Revolution, the advent of mechanical tools, such as large, floor-mounted saw benches, planers, lathes and routers, greatly influenced the sophistication and speed with which prototypes could be made.

Today, the contemporary prototyper falls into one of three categories: those who work exclusively with tools and materials that predate the digital age, those who use digital models and CNC equipment only, and those who employ both. That traditional techniques will eventually be supplanted by the new, digital tools is not inevitable, and remains a matter for the individual designer and their priorities and preferences.

Why even bother to make a distinction between traditional and non-traditional prototyping techniques? The answer is mainly one of context. Before the advent of CNC machinery and its subsequent miniaturization and increased affordability, the manner in which prototyping was undertaken was dependent on the design discipline. In the engineering environment, for example, highly skilled fitters and turners would make working prototypes from the same materials as those intended for the end product. In the industrial designer's workshop, tools typically included soldering irons, small welding equipment, vacuum formers, as well as versions of some of the manufacturing equipment that would be used to make the final, marketed products. Materials ranged from whatever was cheap and easy to work with in order to make visual facsimiles of the intended manufactured item – that is, where only the look and feel of the design was required – to the actual materials to be used for the final product, so that more exacting testing could be carried out. Jewellers also had their own set of specialist tools and techniques, as did all 3D designers, even artists. Architects, however, relied on balsa wood, cardboard and glue. A few practices, such as that of Renzo Piano, were renowned for the central presence in the studio of a woodworking facility, but these were very much the exception.

1. (opposite) Glass-blowing and glass-forming in a steel mould.

2

The advent of inkjet and laser printers, desktop lathes and 3D printers has changed the prototyping landscape considerably, in so far as such digital devices are not discipline-specific, and neither do they demand a specific skill set tied to a particular craft practice, as was the case previously. The use of digital models and CNC tools that can be linked directly to computer files have, to a certain extent, emancipated the designer across all 3D design disciplines. Architects, however, have been the chief beneficiaries; for some, the leap from cardboard mock-ups and prototypes to being able to produce fantastically complex miniature versions of building designs in just a few hours has led to an extraordinary shift in practice.

At a critical level, the extent to which the greatly enhanced opportunities for architects to experiment more vigorously through prototyping have helped inspire spatially and tectonically more sophisticated designs is a question yet to be resolved. Such practices as Foster + Partners, which was already in the habit of prototyping prior to the arrival of the computer, have simply augmented their repertoire. Others, such as dECOi architects, probably developed as conspicuously innovative practices because

of their interest in the role that CNC technologies could play in design experimentation, and the opportunities provided by such equipment to reform architectural practice at a radical level. By contrast, such designers as Thomas Heatherwick demonstrate that contemporary practice need not be in any debt to digital prototyping whatsoever, although this may be the exception that proves the rule: many architects prototype far more now than they did in the past.

2 & 3 (opposite). Goldsmithing in the jeweller's studio.

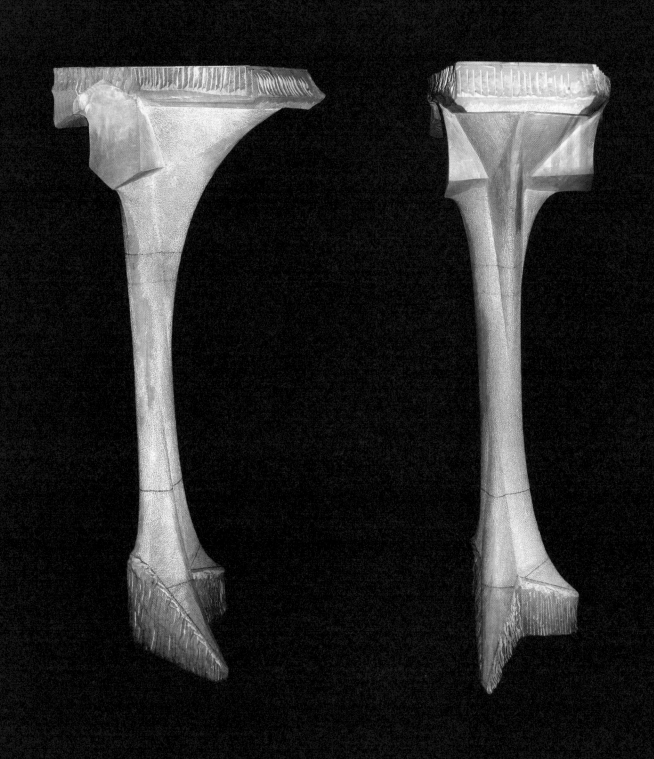

2.2

In Practice →
3.16 / p. 78 / dECOi architects
3.41 / p. 136 / Archi-Union
3.92 / p. 246 / Asif Khan

Mock-ups

1 (opposite). Sagrada Família, Barcelona, Spain, 1882–: 1:5 sandstone version of the first column for the upper colonnade of the Passion Façade, created as a mock-up to review the aesthetics, shadows and fabrication in stone.

In common with the prototype, the mock-up is a type of trial run – a means of testing part of an architectural design prior to construction. Both are aimed at seeking out areas of potential failure in such a design. Although their definitions and applications overlap, every practice approached during the research for this book clearly understood them as serving different purposes. Here we introduce the mock-up as a discrete technique by looking at three kinds of mock-up and their application. The first is the high-fidelity mock-up, which is used late in the design process, primarily as a way to ensure a high-quality build and a good understanding of the sequence of construction. It also provides a last-minute opportunity for design refinement (although this is more a function of the prototype). The second is the low-fidelity, rough, early or 'theatrical' mock-up, which offers none of the detailed exploration of construction and material performance provided by most prototypes, but affords useful ways to explore design concepts and refine the brief. The third is the digital mock-up, where models for the overall geometry of a building and its individual components are brought together to produce a high-fidelity virtual model of the whole assembly.

High-fidelity architectural and construction mock-ups

Since almost all buildings are unique in their layout, structure, composition and the materials from which they are made, there is a strong case for creating mock-ups (high-fidelity facsimiles of small parts of the building) even for relatively conventional designs. Mock-ups are important for identifying failures ahead of time. Building owners often feel that they cannot afford to commission them, although they also expect the final product to be perfect. But quality and precision are almost inevitably achieved only through trial and error, and there is evidence to suggest that it costs more to skip the all-important quality-assurance step that is the mock-up than to include it, despite its potentially disproportionate cost.

There are many compelling and pragmatic reasons for building mock-ups. Structural testing, for example, can highlight problems that are hard to identify purely through calculation and virtual simulation. Testing high-fidelity mock-ups of typical sections of a building envelope (the part of a building separating the internal

2

4–5

3

2–3. Sagrada Família: The mock up of three full-size columns using CNC-carved dense polystyrene foam finished in a render to emulate the surface of granite was outsourced to a fabricator in France. The mock-up was located on-site and used as an aesthetic evaluation tool during the final design of the granite-cut colonnade to come.

4–5. Crowd Productions, spatial and strategic prototyping programme for CUA, Brisbane, Australia, 2012–14: An example of the value of using rapidly made, low-fidelity mock-ups to allow an organization to better understand its spatial needs and how it might improve its own processes – and therefore create a better design brief.

and external environments) can identify its weak points, such as potentially costly energy leaks, and address these in the design and assembly stages. Constructability issues, such as gaining access to the back of a façade to tighten bolts while suspended high in the air, can add significantly to building time and throw out schedules and costs if such issues have not been tackled at the design stage. Mock-ups are a valuable instrument for building contractors, not only for setting standards for the quality of the work carried out across a site, but also for resolving construction-sequencing issues. Mock-ups are also a vital testing ground for the best application of new materials and systems as these enter the construction scene. Depending on the exact nature of the testing, the mock-up may be built on-site or in a certified testing laboratory. If the design being tested is very novel, it may need to be certified for its thermal performance or fire resistance, for instance.

For architects and their clients, mock-ups also provide a final opportunity to review the aesthetics of a particular finish or architectural feature in the actual light and weather conditions on site, or the impact of real deflection under load, at a point in the design process when some refinement is still possible. Designers, building owners and contractors also use mock-ups to compare and evaluate the work of different fabricators as part of the tendering process. Although such mock-ups come late in the process, as high-fidelity renditions of what is to be built, they may also be used to evaluate different design options, particularly in the case of commercial interiors. In this context, it may also be important to be confident that a building's major components and systems – the furniture, joinery, raised floors, cabling, sound masking, access to power and data, movable partitioning and so on, as well as optional layouts and aesthetic decisions – work together to form a coherent whole.

The low-fidelity or 'theatrical' mock-up

In some contexts, 'mock-up' is used to refer to a very early, rough, physical, usually static assemblage intended to investigate or help visualize a speculative design idea. Such a mock-up is close in purpose to a film set or theatrical scenery: an illusory creation not necessarily

6

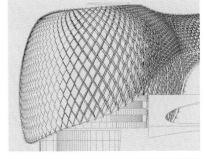

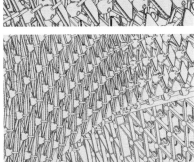

9–10

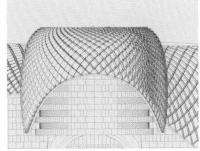

7–8

6. Andrea Palladio, Teatro Olimpico, Vicenza, Italy, 1580–85: For Palladio's theatre, Vincenzo Scamozzi mocked up a long street scene within the depth of the stage, deploying false perspective to create an urban illusion.

7–10. Gehry Technolgies (architects: Asymptote), Yas Viceroy Abu Dhabi hotel, UAE, 2009: The geometrically unique instances of the detailed components and joints from the façade engineers and the developed surface geometry of the whole canopy were combined in a single, computationally heavy digital mock-up to identify and solve any clashes or anomalies before construction.

composed of bona fide materials, or reflecting actual means of construction, but designed to give an otherwise realistic impression of the real thing. A well-known example from Renaissance Italy is the *trompe l'oeil* scenery designed by Vincenzo Scamozzi for Andrea Palladio's Teatro Olimpico (1580–85) in Vicenza, northern Italy, which creates the illusion of streets stretching away to the horizon from three arches at the rear of the stage.

In contrast to the high-fidelity on-site or in-lab construction mock-up – the cost–benefit of which must be weighed up by the client – the low-fidelity theatrical mock-up can be modest in cost, produced in the designer's own studio at an early stage of the design process. It may be an assemblage of materials, a rough structural mock-up that substitutes tubes and sticks for such architectural features as columns and beams, or a full-scale scenographic creation intended to examine human interaction in different spaces, such as commercial, entertainment or hospitality interiors. The props, however, may be the cardboard boxes and broom handles of theatrical rehearsals (see, for example, the work of Crowd Productions, page 254).

Digital mock-ups

The digital mock-up is a computationally heavy virtual model that combines the individual components of a building into a unified whole, thereby allowing any potential problems to be designed out prior to construction. It is particularly useful for testing building envelopes with curving, changing or non-standard geometry that results in families of uniquely shaped and sized components and junctions. Digital mock-ups are virtual mock-ups of the whole design in the tradition of the virtual prototyping undertaken in other industries, such as aircraft and automotive design. To consider a real-world example, digital mock-ups were central to Gehry Technologies' role in the design of the canopy of the Yas Viceroy Abu Dhabi hotel on Yas Island, Abu Dhabi.

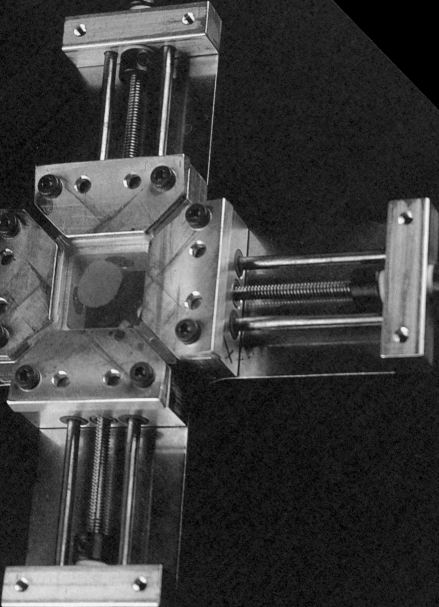

2.3

In Practice →
3.24 / p. 94 / Cloud 9 Architects
3.52 / p. 166 / Hopkins Architects
3.93 / p. 250 / ONL [Oosterhuis_Lénárd]

Prototyping Performance

As the adoption of digital and parametric modelling has become more widespread in both the practice and the teaching of architecture, so too has the recognition that such technologies provide a very tangible opportunity to link architectural models directly to the structural and environmental performance of the finished article through computer simulation – the ability to alter design parameters and observe their impact on design performance. This has simultaneously increased the value of analogue and mixed (i.e. physical and digital) performance prototyping, taking advantage of the increased accessibility of microelectronics for sensing and actuation to link the two.

For multi-criteria optimization, and the exploration of multiple performance criteria and their simultaneous interaction, the level of fidelity and applicability of prototypes – digital, analogue or mixed – is still relatively low. The behaviour of the natural environment is inherently complex; the interaction of light, heat, humidity and air movement, for instance, can have a dynamic and volatile impact on the conditions experienced in a building. Generally speaking, architects use prototyping to gain

feedback and information with which to inform the design process, particularly in the early stages, and are not engaged in the lengthy process of developing more generalizable knowledge about the performance of particular construction systems under particular conditions. Here, we deal briefly with a few examples of prototyping for select performance criteria.

Light and kinetic prototyping

One of the many ways in which the light entering a building can be modulated by means of design is through the introduction of responsive kinetic façades. Kinetic architecture has to be prototyped just to develop robust working kinetic systems. Accurately predicting its environmental performance, in terms of controlling light levels, heat gain and energy use for cooling, and incorporating this into the detailed design of the architecture, adds another complex layer of experimentation and simulation. A well-known example of a building with a kinetic façade designed to respond to and modulate natural lighting and reduce the amount of energy needed to cool the interior

1 (opposite). CASE RPI, Electropolymeric Dynamic Daylighting System (EDDS): Biaxial strain engineering jig.

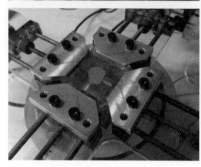

2–4

9–11

5–8

2–8. Electropolymeric Dynamic
Daylighting System (EDDS): Dynamic
strain stage, with a thin sample
of film on a transparent elastomer.

9–11. Sequence of stills from the
full-scale mock-up of the EDDS. The
visual effects are a consequence of
user interaction and environmental
energy modulation.

12–13

14–15

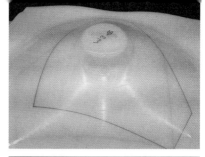
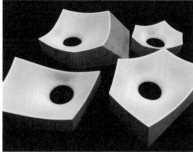

16–17

12–13. SIAL, FabPod meeting room, RMIT University, Melbourne, Australia, 2012–13: Milling a hyperboloid mould using a CNC machine. The doubly curved, ruled hyperboloid surface performs well as a sound diffuser, scattering sound waves.

14–15. Hyperboloid mould for creating spun-aluminium cells for the FabPod.

16. Cutting boundary on hyperboloid in formed acrylic.

17. Unique cells for the assembly of the FabPod. Each cell has the same hyperboloid shape, but the varied boundary shapes and sizes introduce sound-scattering potential, as well as 'organic' visual variety.

is the Institut du Monde Arabe in Paris by Jean Nouvel (completed 1987), with its distinctive, southern-facing brise-soleil grid of camera-shutter oculi. Other examples of kinetic façades include Charles Hoberman and the Adaptive Building Initiative's four 'Intelligent Surfaces' – Tessellate, Permea, Strata and Adaptive Fritting – and the umbrella-like shading system on the Abu Dhabi Investment Council Headquarters by Aedas architects and Arup (completed 2012). While each of these designs is undoubtedly the result of extensive prototyping intended to create a novel working kinetic system, questions remain regarding how to prototype effectively and accurately the actual lighting effects and impact on heating and energy use in the finished buildings.

Acoustics and prototyping

The use of prototyping to evaluate acoustic performance has a long tradition in the design of concert halls and theatres. In the case of such buildings, both large-scale physical (traditionally wooden) models and full-scale wall panels are tested in acoustic laboratory conditions to check predicted reverberation times, clarity and loudness. But such physical models and full-scale mock-ups are expensive and time-consuming to build; moreover, they tend to be employed only once or twice late on in the design process for the purposes of verification or minor refinement. For iterative testing in the more volatile stages of the design process, digital simulation is more affordable and better able to provide the fast analysis turnaround times needed in order effectively to tune the geometry, materiality and mass of a highly acoustically controlled space through trial and error. Computer models for acoustic simulation still need to be simple in shape and polygon count. Such details as the surface shape and materiality of the architecture are approximated by applied digital textures with given attributes – a coarse-grained approximation. There are, however, such initiatives as Arthur van der Harten's Pachyderm plug-in for Rhino 3D (a commercial CAD application) that allow architects to complement the use of costly software packages by expert consultants with more accessible tools, cutting down the analysis time between design iterations in early architectural design.

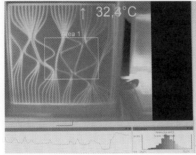

↑ 32,4°C

18–19

20–21

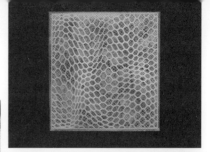

22–23

18–19. Thermal Reticulations research cluster, Smartgeometry, The Bartlett/ UCL, London, 2013: Recording the thermal performance of different façade patterns. Thermal imaging shows the way in which the pattern and materials influence how the surface heats up and cools down, while thermal sensors monitor how heat passes through the façade sample and is distributed in the space behind it.

20–23. Some of the many façade designs, including kinetic systems, that were tested for their thermal performance.

Other sites of acoustic interest for architects include outside high-end performance spaces and the increasingly common phenomenon of open-plan commercial or educational work environments, with their need to accommodate both noisy, collaborative activity and more focused, solitary pursuits within the same space. Using a smorgasbord of media and techniques, the FabPod project (see page 158), for example, was a prototyping exercise intended to investigate the use of geometry and materials to tune the acoustics of a semi-enclosed meeting area.

Air and prototyping

Architecture modulates and controls the temperature and movement of air, shapes internal and external climates, and provides shelter from the extremes of weather. However, although prototyping the interaction between architecture and air is fundamental to architectural design, it is a complex proposition, whether using wind tunnels or computational fluid dynamics. All air is turbulent, even apparently still air in an internal room, and understanding the subtle, site-specific dynamics

of wind and the behaviour of external and internal air in architectural contexts – which is coupled with thermal performance, humidity and air quality in and around buildings – is a complicated business. To really influence the architecture, some understanding is needed through prototyping in the very early stages of design. Fortunately, there is a range of new fluid and thermodynamic simulation software with visualization that architects may find simpler to use than engineering analysis packages. However, each of these applications has limitations that need to be very well understood in order to get any meaningful feedback.

The Tangible Transdisciplinary Table (TTT) is an example of prototyping in 'mixed reality', combining physical modelling and interaction with background digital sensing, simulation and visualization. A so-called demonstrator project, the TTT brought together architects, landscape architects, local planners and engineers around a table on which they could move and interchange building blocks on a city plan and observe changes in a wind simulation projected on to the table in real time. The mixing of physical and virtual prototyping, to provide rapid or near real-

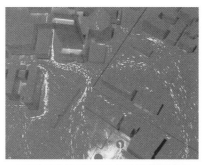

26–27

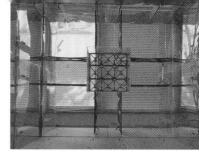

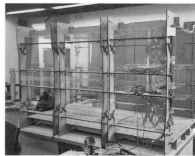

28–29

24–27. Flora Salim *et al.*, Tangible Transdisciplinary Table, RMIT University, Melbourne, Australia, 2013: Simulated wind flow, projected on to the table, alters in real time as designers change the position and shapes of buildings in the model on the table.

28–29. Rafael Moya and Daniel Prohasky, Mini Airflow Tunnel Project: This project is aimed at providing architects with a low-cost platform for rapid wind analysis. Sensors inside a transparent, small-scale wind tunnel evaluate changes in wind speed and pressure, temperature, and humidity when architectural prototypes are placed in the airflow.

time feedback on the impact of design changes, has also proved a powerful way to design for passive thermal and ventilation performance, for instance in the design of building façades.

Prototyping performance in practice

Many of the architectural practices that outlined their use of prototyping for the third part of this book stated strongly that the nature of a prototype depends very much on what is being tested. Among the examples of real-world prototypes described, there are many that were intended to test one aspect of performance in particular, be it structural behaviour, lighting effects or acoustics. Diverse and often complementary means were employed to achieve this aim, some involving the testing of both physical and digital prototypes, some at scale – where it was possible to apply a scaling function to the particular mode of performance – and many at full scale.

2·4

In Practice →
3.22 / p. 88 / Blumer-Lehmann
3.42 / p. 140 / Marble Fairbanks
3.71 / p. 214 / Franken\Architekten

CNC Revolution

With CNC devices, a computer sends instructions directly to a mechanical tool in order to make it perform a specific task. Software interprets a digitally generated design, producing from it a stream of data. The machine at the other end of the process then interprets this data as a set of instructions to undertake a series of actions. Prior to the advent of CNC devices, numerically controlled (NC) machines reacted to instructions sent repeatedly from a storage medium, thereby introducing automation into a manufacturing process that previously had been utterly dependent on direct human agency. The first such automated machines appeared in the mid-twentieth century, having evolved from earlier semi-automated machines that were managed using punched tape or punched cards.

At its most basic, a CNC device might consist of a cutting blade that can be made to move in one dimension. The CNC revolution began properly, however, with the introduction of three-dimensional control, with a fourth dimension being the finely controlled displacement of the crafting tool in one, two or all three dimensions in a given period of time.

The 'control' aspect of CNC devices is dependent on the use of the stepper motor. Whereas a brushed direct-current motor performs an indefinite number of revolutions while a current is applied, the stepper motor moves a precise fraction of a revolution, or step, per electrical pulse. If the motor has been set up to complete a single revolution in 200 steps, for example, each motor step will be a rotation of 1.8 degrees. Using a computer, much finer movement can be achieved through 'microstepping', with some motors able to perform as many as 50,000 steps per revolution, making each step equivalent to 0.0072 degrees. In sending its instructions as a wave of pulses, the computer can determine not only the number of steps in a rotation but also the speed of that rotation; this it does by simply changing the interval between pulses in the respective information stream. With separate stepper motors controlling movement in the X-, Y- and Z-axes, each might receive different numbers of pulses at different intervals. In this way, movement in space can be very precisely controlled, in terms of both position and speed. Being able to control the speed of a CNC device is crucial: there is no point, for example, in trying

1 (opposite). A stepper motor, the basic ingredient of computer numerical control (CNC) devices. The motor rotates by a precise number of degrees per computer-generated 'pulse'.

2–3

4–5

2–3. Two examples of multi-axis robotic stone cutting. While the robot arm (seen on the left-hand side of each photograph) has fives axes of movement, the elevating turntable in the top image provides a further two axes.

4–5. The automobile industry has helped lead the way in the use of fully automated manufacturing processes. The building industry, however, has lagged behind, with on-site digital assembly yet to reach the same level of sophistication as off-site digital fabrication.

to push a router bit through a sheet of plywood faster than the router can cut the material.

Beyond the precision of the stepper motor – an invention that, although it dates from the nineteenth century, did not reach the necessary level of controllability until the 1950s – is the issue of feedback from the task being performed. Today, the sophisticated use of CNC devices depends on the ability to interact with and adjust the programmed stream of information from the computer in reaction to error or such uncontrollable factors as variations in the material.

The makers of architectural prototypes are essentially interested in three types of CNC: 'subtractive', using cutters and routers (see page 41); 'additive', using machine-guided depositors of materials (see page 45); and fully robotic, which might include both additive and subtractive techniques (see page 49). Cutters are used to produce shapes from flat sheets. Routers, on the other hand, although they too can convert flat material into 2D shapes, are more usefully employed producing 3D objects from a mass of raw material. Routers include a subclass of lathes, where

a cutting tool works horizontally on a fast-spinning piece of sculpturing material. CNC depositors, meanwhile, produce small objects by means of the deposition of material with extreme precision.

Cutting templates can require more than two dimensions of movement – for example, if a thick sheet of material needs a slanted cut. Also, if a 3D object being milled or routed requires an undercut, more than three degrees of freedom and operation are required. As a consequence, reference is often made to the 'five-axis router', used to cut flat sheets of material, and 'seven-axis robots', used to mill complex 3D objects. Clearly, today's machines are required to be far more sophisticated than the simple 'XY' cutter invented at MIT in 1952. The programs that determine where a cutting head is in space at a particular point in time have to calculate the optimum, most time-efficient cutting paths in anticipation of the desired outcome. Furthermore, highly sophisticated awareness has to be built in, to enable the device to make real-time adjustments in line with feedback from sensors, and to allow for the weight and momentum of different machine

6–7

8–9

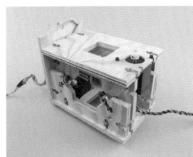

10–11

6–9. SuperStrusion, RMIT Industrial Design, Melbourne, Australia, 2014: The SuperStrusion studio was set up to develop and build unique extruder heads for use in a 3D printer. In particular, the aim was to explore the printer's capacity to build innovative objects using such unusual materials as plasticine, wax, chocolate, ice-cream, expanding foam and cookie dough.

10–11. DIYLILCNC, Chicago, IL, 2012: The DIYLILCNC project is composed of a free and open-source set of plans for an inexpensive, fully functional three-axis CNC mill that can be built by any individual who has basic workshop skills and tool access.

heads. It must also have anti-clashing capability, so that it does not impede its own operation.

Prior to automation, all machines involved in the manufacturing cycle were operated by hand. Considerable levels of skill were needed on the part of the machine operators, especially in the manufacture of precision parts, thereby putting considerable distance between the maker and the designer. In the context of architecture, there was a triangular relationship between the designer, the craftsperson and the mechanical tool used to fashion the desired architectural component. With the introduction of sophisticated CNC, however, the craftsperson is no longer necessarily a part of that relationship: in theory, equipped with the right software, the designer can produce their design simply by pressing the 'enter' key on their computer and letting the CNC device do the rest. Such a scenario is still some way off, in part because there is still a vast gap between the skills required to use CAD software, and those needed to work with such CNC programming languages as the ubiquitous G-code. But things are changing. Efforts are being made by the manufacturers of CNC machines, for example,

to simplify their programming, and there are already many architects fully able to program their own robots with minimal technical support. Schools of architecture too are actively adapting their curricula in order to accommodate a degree of skill acquisition in this field. Architectural students engaging with the means of production so explicitly represents a quantum leap in thinking compared with previous generations, and it is somewhat ironic that rather than technology further distancing the designer from the making process, quite the opposite seems to be happening.

2·5

In Practice →
3.31 / p. 106 / designtoproduction
3.46 / p. 156 / SIAL
3.74 / p. 224 / Jordi Faulí

Prototyping Through Subtraction

The use of CNC devices in manufacturing has introduced two new techniques for the prototyping of architectural design: material subtraction and material addition. With instructions emanating from the designer's computer, linked robots, routers, lasers, plasma streams and water jets can cut away at material through abrasive, burning or evaporative subtraction. This 'material subtraction', as the process is known, is the counterpart to 'material addition', a completely distinct process that is covered in the next section (see page 45).

Semi- and fully automated manufacturing has a relatively short history, and it was not until the 1970s that the use of CNC devices became widespread. It was in the late 1990s, however, that the miniaturization of computing – and thus the dawn of the personal computer – converged with the miniaturization and increased user-friendliness of CNC-driven tools. For the first time since the beginning of the industrial age, designers became properly empowered, no longer having to send designs for prototyping out to specialists. Design studios with a strong interest in modelling, prototyping and mocking-up within the curtilage of their own offices could benefit from the making happening sufficiently close to the designing. The speed with which a design could be fashioned and tested on-site afforded far greater sophistication than ever before, leading to the creation of a genuine critical-feedback loop.

Of particular note is the term 'rapid prototyping', which for the designer means not having to wait very long between coming up with a concept and a physical realization of that concept being available for appraisal. It also means a greater chance of being able to make affordable working prototypes from the materials to be used for the built design, giving earlier insight into the viability of an idea.

There are two different methods of material subtraction using CNC machinery. The first, cutting, can be done with a fast-turning router bit, or by laser-beam burning (as opposed to sintering), plasma stream, water jet, spark erosion (electric-discharge machining) or electrophoresis. All these technologies rely on a CNC machine that can move the cutting device in the X–Y plane, for simple sheet cutting, or, for slanted cuts, along the X-, Y- and Z-axes. A router bit can make contoured, '2½D' objects from thicker

1 (opposite). A five-axis CNC router at work. The cutting head can move in two dimensions (X and Y), elevate (Z), and rotate around both X and Y axes, allowing the machine to make slanted cuts as well as undercuts.

2-3

4

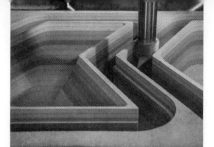

5-6

2-3. A five-axis router carves elements for a roofing prototype.

4. designtoproduction, iBAR: A CNC milling machine is used to create a 1:10-scale prototype.

5-6. AL_A, Cork Kit, Experimentadesign Biennial, Lisbon, 2013.

sheets of material; when working with such low-cost materials as polystyrene blocks, the contouring can be especially pronounced. The second method of material subtraction, grinding or milling, is generally done with a router or saw blade attached to a robot arm, rather than a 2D frame. In some cases, this arm gives the grinding or sawing head equal reach along all three axes. Even large pieces of stone, measuring several metres in height, width and depth, can now be whittled away using a seven-axis CNC robot arm.

Material subtraction takes place at two distinct scales of operation: industrial and workshop. Obviously, rendering a large block of stone is not within the capabilities of a typical design studio, but it is now possible for smaller-scale rendering to take place in a studio workshop or even on a desktop. In the mid-1990s, miniature CNC routing devices began to appear on the market, bringing the benefits enjoyed by industry within the designer's grasp. Before long, astonishingly precise chess pieces, for example, began to be shown around design offices, pointing to a different future than the one most designers might have imagined.

Unfortunately, the rhetoric was more powerful than the reality, and several factors conspired to limit their impact: cost, noisiness in operation, the production of a large quantity of offcuts and shavings, a limited range of sculpting materials, and a relative lack of speed. Nevertheless, the miniature and rapid-prototyping genie had been let out of the bottle, and, almost simultaneously, machines for depositing materials became available. Although initially these were not desktop-sized, they could at least be incorporated into a typical prototyping and modelling workshop.

Perhaps the most startling innovation in the introduction of CNC prototyping into the designer's realm were the laser cutters that began to appear in progressive design schools and professional studios in the late 1990s. Typically able to cut a sheet of material up to A1 in size, such machines could produce miraculously accurate shapes at great speed. Although they were aimed more at the model-maker, anyone wishing to craft a volume from flat or developable surfaces were being offered a real gift. At first there were technical difficulties around exhaust gases and a constant need

7–8

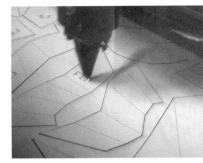

9–10

11–12

7. Franken\Architekten, Home Couture, Berlin, Germany, 2005: For the street façade of Home Couture, the first Raab Karcher flagship store, CNC milling was used to create glass with unique optical properties.

8. A water-jet cutter in action.

9–12. BKK Architects, design for *Pavilions of New Architecture*, Monash University Museum of Art (MUMA), Melbourne, Australia, 2005: Laser cutting and assembly of the bespoke structural components.

to clean and re-calibrate, but these issues have been resolved to the extent that such machines are now ubiquitous.

For those wishing to create prototypes from such sheet materials as cardboard, Perspex, polyurethane and polycarbonate, the studio-based laser cutter more than answers their needs, especially in terms of a rapid turnaround. The more 'serious' materials – glass, metals, ceramics – are cut using the more challenging technologies, such as water-jet and plasma-stream cutting, which can work on sheets of surprising thickness. Altough these technologies are unlikely to be found in the prototyper's studio, prototyping designers know about them and exploit their capabilities when appropriate.

At the time of writing, there is a sense that CNC cutting and routing tools, along with their associated software, have reached a certain maturity whereby they can be engaged with experimentally. That is to say, educators can act with confidence in introducing their students to the opportunities these devices offer: rather than being a passing interest, they, like the computers that control them, seem to point to a future of more sophisticated prototyping,

as well as equally sophisticated off-site fabrication. Together with simplified programming, the miniaturization of subtractive systems means that such tools as full-sheet-size (240 × 120-cm) cutters can augment the workshop of every school of architecture. With wider access to such resources, the pavilion-scale prototypes that have been emerging from the Institute for Computational Design (ICD) in Stuttgart, the Centre for Information Technology and Architecture (CITA) in Copenhagen, the Architectural Association School of Architecture in London and the Spatial Information Architecture Laboratory (SIAL) in Melbourne will soon begin appearing in all parts of the world.

2·6

In Practice →
3.23 / p. 90 / Bollinger + Grohmann
3.63 / p. 192 / Francis Bitonti
3.84 / p. 238 / Greg Lynn

Prototyping Through Addition

Prototyping through addition, or additive prototyping, refers to the creation of prototypes from digital files by means of the deposition of a particular material. There are several types of additive prototyping, and the technology is rapidly spawning not only new varieties of materials with which to make '3D prints', but also machines that can print using more than one material. Depending on the material used, the amount of preparation of the digital model prior to printing varies, as does the amount of post-printing finishing that is required.

The simplest form of additive prototyping involves the sectioning of the digital model into a specified number of layers, which are then deposited on a platen in the form of thin films of dust. As each layer of dust is deposited, the material is fused into a solid, either through the spraying of glue or other liquid matrix, or by the accurate pointing of a laser. In this way, the print builds up incrementally, layer by layer, until the object has been fully formed. Post-printing requires the removal of all the residual, un-fused material for reuse, while porous materials may need binding to make them more robust. Materials used for 3D printing range

from the relatively cheap (and fragile), such as wax (discussed in more detail below) and plaster of Paris, to more the expensive, i.e. metals; in-between is a rapidly expanding range of plastics, rubbers and resins. The most common printing materials currently in use are such thermoplastics as PLA and ABS, which are relatively cheap and quick to use. They tend to produce quite 'clunky' objects, but they can also be used to make working prototypes for testing physical feasibility. Increasingly, with the technology evolving at tremendous speed, additive prototyping can be used to create working prototypes from the materials to be used for the final, built design, or their equivalents at least in terms of strength. For architects in the mould of Jean Prouvé, this represents an extraordinary boost to their opportunities to experiment with a greater sense of confidence about the viability of the final outcome.

A second form of additive prototyping uses light to cure liquid into a solid, such as in stereolithography. In common with other forms of additive prototyping, the required structure is built up layer by layer, in this case from a liquid polymer that hardens on contact with the light

1 (opposite). ThermoJet 3D printing using wax as the extruded modelling medium. This example – a model of the 'ribs' for one of the four towers at the Sagrada Família in Barcelona dedicated to the evangelists – demonstrates the delicacy and precision that can be achieved with wax-based 3D printing. It also shows the large amounts of support structure that have to be removed and disposed of once the model has cooled.

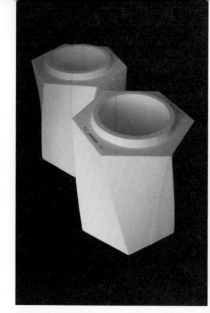

2

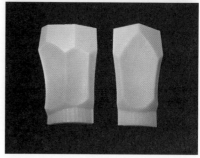

4–5

3

46

2. Drainpipe elements from the nave of the Sagrada Família, printed in 2002. The arrival of 3D printers in the architect's studio enabled the robust and rapid prototyping of even the most prosaic of building components.

3. With wax-based 3D printing, a significant amount of the expensive and non-recyclable medium is used for 'support structures', as can be seen here. Removing the strands of unwanted wax can take as much time as printing the object in the first place.

4–5. Notwithstanding the costs associated with early wax-based 3D printers, such machines offered architects the opportunity to produce accurate manifestations of their ideas at a speed previously unheard of.

from a computer-controlled laser beam. This was one of the earliest forms of additive prototyping, and is still used widely for very accurate reproductions. Owing to the way the object is formed, micro support structures are needed to hold the hardening model as it cures; post-production, these supports have to be carefully removed. However, continuing improvements in both the processes involved and the chemicals used mean that this previously time-consuming practice is on the wane.

While 3D printing was first used for rapid prototyping in the early 1980s, albeit in a very primitive form, it was not until the late 1990s that architects were able to access such radical new technology. Typically adopted from the aeronautical and automotive industries, which were using it for the full-scale prototyping of mechanical widgets and articulations, 3D printing slowly became a highly valued yet costly means of producing scaled models for architects – the actual usefulness of that scale for architectural terms being a moot point.

The advantages of 3D printing include the ability to produce highly detailed objects (regardless of scale) accurately and at great speed, as compared to the traditional craft processes that the new technology is beginning to replace. In a matter of hours, the designer can have in their hands a highly precise and finished physical representation of something that had previously existed only on their computer screen. But there are disadvantages too, some of which have disappeared during the first fifteen years of take-up, and some of which have not.

Principal among the most recent developments in 3D printing are the arrival of new types of media and a reduction in costs. For the first few years of the technology, the architect had the option of printing additively in wax, rather than robotically milling their design from a block of suitable material (as outlined in the previous section). The wax, however, was expensive to procure – a point of irritation for many, as despite the manufacturers' claims to the contrary, it bore a close resemblance to the type of wax used for church candles. As it was, the nozzles of the printers became blocked far too frequently using the correct material; any warranty in this regard would have been instantly voided were the use of unorthodox material discovered.

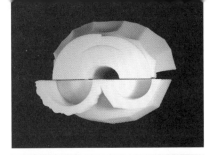

6–7

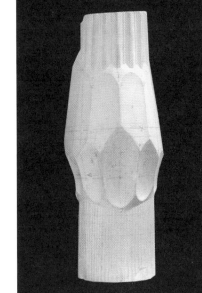

8

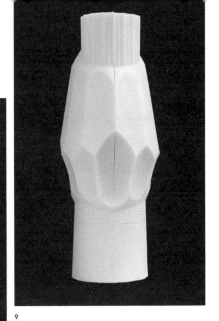

9

6–9. Further examples, from 2001, of ThermoJet 3D printing using wax as the medium. The objects themselves are models of the upper and lower halves of the node where the nave columns of the Sagrada Família divide into two.

A significant proportion of the wax was wasted through the construction of elaborate 'support structures' beneath the still-solidifying object above, which would otherwise be in danger of collapsing under its own weight. Moreover, it generally took as many hours to clean and 'post-process' the object as it did to print it. The first two tasks involved manually stripping away the supports (which, according to the manufacturers at least, could not be recycled) and glass-bead blasting the surface with care and precision. The first wax-based 3D printers cost more than $100,000, and required regular servicing by specialists. They were also unable to produce objects larger than 20 cm (7¾ in.) in any direction, which for architects meant producing models either in several parts or whole but at a very small scale. In warm climates, models would perceptibly change shape over the years, to the extent that taking dimensions from them was foolhardy. And, being wax, the models could not be painted.

As soon as the so-called dust printers described above came on to the market, the desirability of the wax printer disappeared almost overnight. It is highly likely that many investors and early adopters saw their machines being mothballed before reaching the end of their useful lives. Amortizing such investments, however, is a risky business. The technology has not yet joined the typewriter or steam engine, and as anyone working as a jeweller or in the dental industry will tell you, these highly precise 3D printers have no equal when it comes to producing models for lost-wax casting.

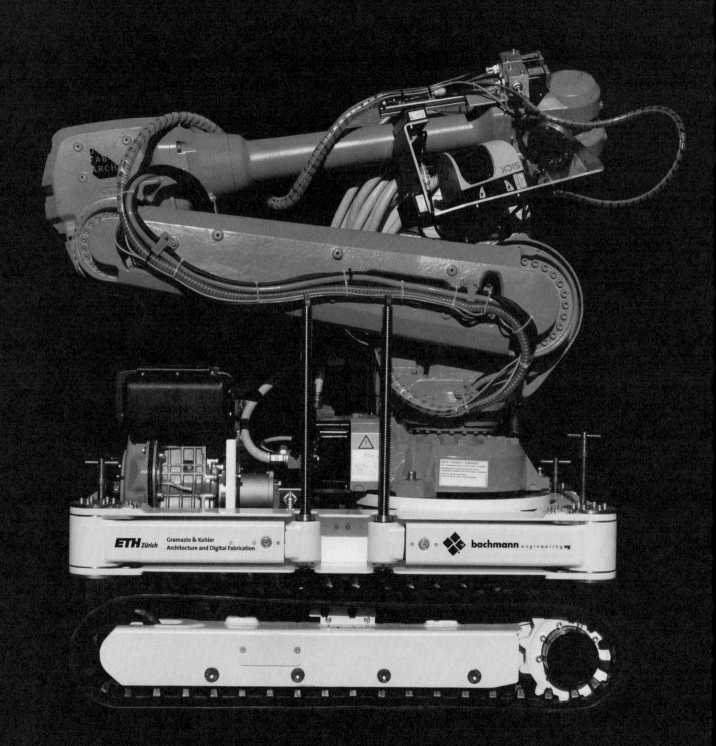

2·7

In Practice →
3.66 / p. 204 / AL_A
3.72 / p. 218 / ICD
3.91 / p. 242 / Foster + Partners

Enter the Robot

Industrial robots have transformed the world of manufacturing. Among other things, they are extremely versatile. Compared to 3D printers and such flat-bed CNC machines as laser cutters and three- and even five-axis milling machines, the articulated robot arm offers much greater freedom in terms of how an operation may be executed. Moreover, in contrast to most CNC devices, which are developed specifically for a single type of operation – whether that be laser cutting or printing a particular material or combination of materials – robots can provide a platform for just about any operation conceivable. By fitting a robot with different tools (or 'end effectors'), the same basic machine can be used to mill, drill, pick up and place, print, cut, draw, stack, unload, inspect (with a camera), or weld, to name but a few of the possible operations. Naturally, and especially since the growth of the market and the fall in prices, robots have become an attractive proposition not only for researchers, who are keen to explore their potential in a variety of disciplines, but also for a small but growing number of architectural practices, which are installing robots in their workshops. Previously, whenever these

same practices required bespoke architectural objects, they had to collaborate with specialist, robot-employing fabricators. The authors of the present book, for instance, have been involved with outsourced robotic stone-cutting at the Sagrada Família in Barcelona since 1992.

Robots are not simply about enhancing productivity or precision. In common with CNC machines in general, they can perform in ways that reveal new creative opportunities. One of the first projects to open the eyes of the architectural world to such opportunities was Gramazio Kohler's 'informed wall' of 2006, an architectonic brick wall laid by a robot. However, despite the wider application of robotics in construction, particularly civil engineering projects, the uptake in architecture has been relatively slow: by 2010 robots were still rare in both education and professional practice. There are sound reasons for this. Controlling the movement of robots requires considerable skill and expertise, which meant that, initially, their use was confined to the realm of such specialist architectural and engineering bodies as Gramazio Kohler, ETH Zurich and Robots in Architecture at Vienna University of Technology.

1 (opposite). A robot from the robotic fabrication laboratory of Swiss architectural practice Gramazio Kohler. With their many articulated joints giving them a human quality, and regardless of size or function, robots have a special place in the affections of makers.

2–3

4–5

6–7

2–7. Gramazio Kohler, 'Acoustic Bricks', non-standard acoustic panel system, ETH Zurich, 2012–14: In the 'Acoustic Bricks' project, a robot was used to fabricate an acoustic wall system for office spaces.

Indeed, the Swiss architectural practice of Gramazio Kohler remains at the forefront of research into robotic fabrication. The project 'Acoustic Bricks' (2012–14), for example, was focused on the robotic fabrication of an acoustic wall system for office spaces. The aims of the project were twofold: first, the incorporation of a powerful but rarely recognized acoustical phenomenon, sound diffusion, into the making of the proposed walls; and secondly, the development of a computational design and fabrication framework that would allow the production of individually adaptable walls in an industrial context.

When the constraints on their mobility have been neither fully understood nor correctly programmed, robots represent a much greater risk to the user than other CNC machines. They are potentially very powerful beasts, which, once in operation, will follow the paths dictated to them by their programming with limited real-time feedback. Proximity sensing is used to protect people and robots from actual collisions, but will not guard against the possibility of an only slightly mis-programmed robot attempting to create, say, a fused deposition model on

the ceiling. But faced with an almost infinite number of ways in which a robotic arm can move, describing the spatial constraints of a given task and the impact of this on a design in progress is far from easy.

The traditional workflow was cumbersome. Recent work on the use of robots in architectural design and production, however, has focused on developing control environments that allow the designer to work directly within their chosen (parametric) design environment and incorporate the spatial and sequencing constraints of the robot into the design. This replaces the much more complicated feedback systems that used computer-aided manufacturing (CAM) software to consider the tool and its holder moving in space but not the robot and its own constraints. Multiple inspection routines to ensure that the tool could reach the design and did not collide with it, and a robot simulation to optimize the placement of the design relative to the robot, have been superseded by an integrated, informed design environment. As a result, feedback on what can be accomplished, and how, is immediate, and can be used to inform the design process.

8–9

10–11

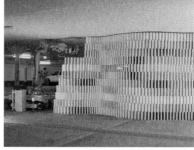

12–13

8–13. Gramazio Kohler, 'Echord', *in situ* robotic fabrication, ETH Zurich, 2011–12: With the 'Echord' project, the objective was for the robot to be able to respond to different construction tolerances and adapt to changing conditions autonomously. The end goal is the direct employment of industrial robots on the construction site.

The word 'robot' (from *robota*, the Czech for 'forced labour') has its origins in the world of science fiction – specifically, a 1920 play by the Czech writer Karel Capek. In the real world, robots have been playing a part in manufacturing – and even construction – for several decades. The robot arm in its current form was developed in the 1970s, and was common in manufacturing by the mid-1980s, notably in the Japanese car industry. Robots, however, have predominantly been used to carry out repetitive operations with great precision, and are expensive to retool and recalibrate for different tasks, with the viability of each new tool path having to be checked. Consequently, their appeal to architects, who are working in the realm of customized and bespoke production with a wide range of materials, remains limited. Nevertheless, the benefits offered by robotics – including an almost unlimited freedom of movement and the ability to perform such tasks as flank milling, which reduces the number of subtractive operations needed and the amount of waste material produced – will continue to attract the architectural prototyping community to robots as co-creators.

2.8

In Practice →
3.32 / p. 110 / Arup
3.44 / p. 146 / SHoP
3.73 / p. 222 / SUPERSPACE

Virtual Prototyping

In virtual prototyping, the prototype exists as a digital simulation only. It can be a 2D diagram, a 3D model and animation, or an interactive 4D model that can be manipulated in real time. As we will see in Part 3, the importance of virtual prototyping to the architectural community varies considerably between practices, with some treating it as central to their work, and others using it in combination with other types of prototyping. Crucially, the virtual prototype is different from the digital mock-up (see page 29): while the latter is a representation of the finished article, the former is used to represent specific attributes of a given design.

Originally, virtual prototyping was developed for the engineering sector. As the computational assessment of structural performance grew more reliable, designers were able to dispense with the expensive and time-consuming practice of testing physical prototypes – of engine components, for example – to destruction. In particular, a combination of such techniques as finite element analysis (FEA) and genetic algorithms has given engineers sufficient assurance to be able to reduce radically the amount of material used in certain structures.

In architecture, the growth in kinetic and adaptive designs has seen a corresponding increase in the need for performance prototyping (see page 31). Here, virtual prototyping has enabled architects to progress their designs far further along the development track before having to hand over to specialist engineers and manufacturers. It has also reduced the extent to which architects need to involve themselves in the computational aspects of design, with basic analysis being incorporated into the design tools. Architects are now able to evaluate the degree (and type) of curvature, for example, as part of their considerations around choice of material.

The transition from analogue simulation to the greater versatility of the digital variety has been fascinating. The eight years that Gaudí spent on developing his design for the Church of Colònia Güell on the outskirts of Barcelona using a 1:10 scaled model attests to the innate desire of architects to understand the performative aspects of their designs. Virtual prototyping affords the Gaudís of this world an opportunity to start thinking about designing with a real-time feedback loop to support the crucial task of performative decision-making.

A rendering of the Times Eureka Pavilion, Kew Gardens, London, UK, 2011, designed by Nex— in collaboration with the landscape designer Marcus Barnett.

Prototypes in Practice

There are wry smiles among architects and designers when a client or stakeholder says, 'But why did you not show us this version before?' Good design is a process, sometimes a lengthy and arduous one, and it is only through this process that the final design will reveal itself to its maker. Designing is sometimes represented as a conversation – an interrogation, even – not only between participants but also between the designer and their own incomplete, partial representation of the design in its nascent form, speaking back to its author. The prototype is one of the tools that allow designers to think and feel their way into a design and seek feedback from it. What the designers whose practice is explored in this section have in common is that they build versions of the design, or aspects of it, in order to find their way further into the design process: components or materials should come together, a feeling they are trying to evoke, a quality of detail, or even an abstract concept or principal of assembly that will ultimately appear in more than one project. For each of the featured designers, there is a deep emotional and aesthetic aspect to this search-through-making that transcends purely analytical understanding – a hunt for the ineffable that lifts the final design to a point that will resonate and speak to hearts beyond that of its creator. In its making, in some cases by hand, the prototype enables the designer to think and feel their way more deeply into their design.

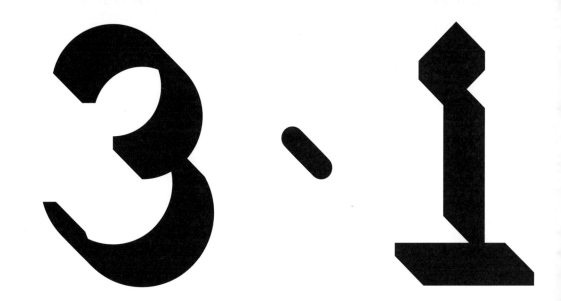

A Tool for Thinking / Feeling

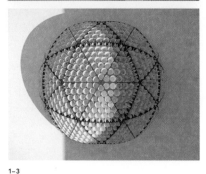

1–3

3 · 11

← Techniques
2.1 / p. 23 / Traditional Techniques
2.2 / p. 27 / Mock-ups

Rory Hyde

A 'baggy' tool for thinking/convincing oneself

For Australian architect Rory Hyde, author of the prize-winning book *Future Practice: Conversations from the Edge of Architecture* (2012), a prototype is something that is intentionally 'baggy', meaning adaptable and loose. Hyde believes that while designers use models to convince others, a prototype is an internal tool for convincing oneself.

The iconic, low-cost Ikea rubbish bin as an architectural component seems a natural choice for a designer who espouses a broader, more public conversation in architecture. But its adoption for the 'Bin Dome', an installation for the exhibition *Melbourne Now* (2013–14), has a more subtle backstory. Its site was Federation Court, originally an open courtyard, now glazed over, in Roy Grounds's iconic National Gallery of Victoria (1968), one of several arts buildings on Melbourne's south bank. The dome and its bins make reference to a series of homemade, exploratory prototypes built by Grounds on a rural property in Penders on the south coast of New South Wales. One of these was a version of Buckminster Fuller's geodesic dome. The military precision of Fuller's dome was reinterpreted by Grounds in the 'she'll-be-right' setting of an Australian backyard using driftwood and, for the structural nodes, the then ubiquitous galvanized dustbin lid. Hyde's Ikea rubbish bins are a 'nod to that kind of sensibility', taking a generic object to 'slap together'.

In reality, the very elegant 'Bin Dome' was the product of six months of relentless prototyping and the careful, experimental assembly of bins. Initially, these were represented with polystyrene drinking cups, but were

1–3. 'Bin Dome', *Melbourne Now*, National Gallery of Victoria, Melbourne, Australia, 2013–14: Renderings from the digital model of the whole assembly, displaying the configuration of the primary elements within the space of the gallery.

4–5. Initial concept sketches exploring the geometrical opportunities for organizing structure and bins on the surface of a spherical dome, and the components needed to assemble them.

6–8. Initial prototypes of a single triangular module, already requiring tricky angle cuts to assemble correctly. This was an important aesthetic test.

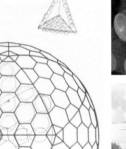

$k = \sqrt{\frac{1}{4} + \left(\frac{1}{8}\right)^2}$

$\gamma =$

$> \frac{\sqrt{5} + 1}{2}$

$= 1.618$

$\gamma = 1.618 = \left(\frac{1}{8}\right)$

$-1.$

$\gamma - 1 = \frac{1}{8}$

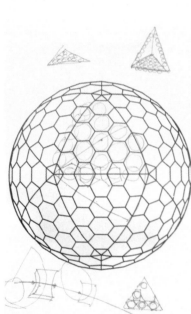

4–5

6–8

9–12

9–12. 'Bin Dome': Four triangular modules are assembled into the next scale of module (figs 9–10). Later, the main dome structure is assembled off-site to check the junctions between structural members, as well as the entry arches at the base of the dome (figs 11–12).

13–14

15–16

17–18

60

13–14. 'Bin Dome': A customizable jig is used to manufacture the fifteen identical 5-metre-long laminated veneer lumber (LVL) beams on the correct arc.

15–16. Building the triangular infill panels.

17–18. The initial stages of installation at the National Gallery of Victoria, using minimal scaffolding.

quickly replaced with full-scale triangular panels of bins approximately 2 metres across. Hyde refers to a moment in every project when, by getting a small piece of it to work at 1:1 scale, you soon realize that the rest of it will work too. Hyde's full-scale blue whale of electroluminescent wire – *Meet Your Energy Avatar*, made in collaboration with Katja Novitskova for the exhibtion *New Order* (2012) at Mediamatic in Amsterdam – was another case in point. Getting the electronic specifications right for 2 metres meant understanding the circuit diagram for the entire, 40-metre-long whale.

The 'she'll-be-right' approach was quickly abandoned in the 'Bin Dome' prototyping process. Mitring the triangular frames for the panels, for example, required an off-45-degree angle not easily accomplished with a drop saw at home; however, in order to ensure that the frames would hold without breaking, the precise angle had to be achieved early on. Originally, each bin was to act as a plant container, with the soil required for the plants adding 2–10 kilograms per bin to the overall structure. But the resulting droop and loss of translucency seen in the early prototypes drove the designers to the air-plant solution: bromeliads and other epiphytes that live on the surface of trees.

While the original vision was a structural dome consisting purely of bins, the scale of the project required an independent structure made of laminated veneer lumber (LVL) assembled from high-grade 15-millimetre plywood. The fifteen beams that make up the structure are identical, 5-metre-long arcs, which can be documented in two A4 drawings and

19

20–21

a template for hole cutting. The openness of the dome, however, guarantees uneven loads, causing up to 10 millimetres of deflection and shift – movements the designers noticed and worried about during construction, but which were no longer apparent when all the bins were in place. The prototyping never ceased, even during the final construction phase, with questions being asked about bolt details, cut-outs, which parts to paint, how to glue a plant in, which of three glues holds and colours least, and so on. Prior to actual construction, the only complete views of the dome were digital.

The original commission from the gallery was to reproduce an earlier installation: a dome of umbrellas. Hyde, however, had in his mind the more site-specific 'Bin Dome', and received a quarter of the total budget to prototype the untested design and produce a proof of concept for the gallery to approve. The physical prototyping also provided useful information for the beam fabricators; indeed, many fabricators still do not use digital-modelling software. But what, in Hyde's view, is the most important thing tested by prototypes? 'Whether [a design] is good enough … Whether it elicits the right emotive response. You think you are just testing the junctions but you are actually testing your own faith in it.'

19. 'Bin Dome': Interior view of the completed pavilion.

20–21. Exterior views of the completed pavilion, with the bromeliads and other epiphytes in place.

1–3

3·12

← Techniques
2.1 / p. 23 / Traditional Techniques
2.2 / p. 27 / Mock-ups

HYBRIDa [Jordi Truco / Sylvia Felipe]

Thinking as doing: doing as thinking

Jordi Truco and Sylvia Felipe, partners in the Barcelona-based practice HYBRIDa, claim 'thinking as doing' as their approach to architecture and design. It is an open, exploratory framework within which they try to discover what is going to happen through a cycle of making and testing. They credit their time on the Emergent Technologies and Design (EmTech) programme at the Architectural Association in London, following a more classical education at the Barcelona School of Architecture (ETSAB), with feeding their appetite for this kind of adventurous and investigative practice.

It was prototypes that won HYBRIDa funding from the European Union for the research project Hypermembrane. The practice, however, makes prototypes for every project, never just models. This distinguishes them, says Truco, from those architects and designers who 'do not want to make prototypes because they make you sort out many, many things'. A prototype has to test performance, and in the case of Hypermembrane, the form was determined by the detailed performance of the materials.

There were days when the architects were discussing with Ascamm, one of the six other partners in the European consortium involved in the project, how big the machine should be to make the composite material for Hypermembrane's musculature. What pressure would it require? How many wires should be in the material? At such times, the architects would begin to feel that they were straying too far from what it was they had set out to achieve. But Ascamm too were charting the unknown and relying on feedback from the things they were making to inform their ideas.

1–3. Hypermembrane: A proposal for the Salamanca Sport Stadium, Spain.

4–7

8–11

12–15

4–7. The telescopic supports and footing fixings of a Hypermembrane.

8–15. Hypermembrane: 'Skinning' an early prototype frame.

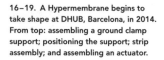

16–19

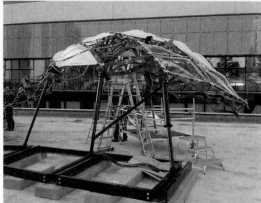

20–21

16–19. A Hypermembrane begins to take shape at DHUB, Barcelona, in 2014. From top: assembling a ground clamp support; positioning the support; strip assembly; and assembling an actuator.

20–21. Assembling the membrane cushions at DHUB.

Unless you understand prototyping as a process in which ideas and making inform one another, believes Truco, you will see only a product, not the opportunity to experiment and create something new.

Although scale is important when talking about Hypermembrane – an experiment in the physics of a modular system capable of changing its shape to fit almost any architectural context – it is essentially scaleless: the size of the individual modules is determined by material and production parameters. A series of 1:5 prototypes provided some information about the system's behaviour, while full-scale prototyping was essential for understanding the performance of the moving parts that drive its complex reconfigurations. Moving any part of the structure results in a redistribution of load in every other part. However, at its present scale (a grid of 100 by 100 nodes), it is not possible to predict performance, so a real-time feedback system is needed to avoid any load concentrations that may lead to damage. Simulations of the system in action were conducted with the International Center for Numerial Methods in Engineering (CIMNE).

What, then, makes Hypermembrane a prototype? 'Easy', replies Truco. 'Hypermembrane is a prototype because it is not yet ready for industrialization. It is a little bit closer to production than any other system that produces complex morphologies, but it still sits in-between.' Eventually, the aim is to explore real-time dynamics: how, for example, might the structure respond to the changing seasons?

22–24

25–26

23–26. Views of the completed
Hypermembrane at DHUB.

1–2

3·13

← Techniques
2.1 / p. 23 / Traditional Techniques
2.2 / p. 27 / Mock-ups

MAD Architects

Prototyping an idea or feeling to give it form

To the Beijing-based practice of MAD Architects, architecture is a quest to find and communicate a 'feeling'. In common with the depiction of bamboo in a traditional Chinese painting, it is not the architecture per se that is important, but rather the feelings of the architect and how these are communicated to others in the subsequent experience of the work. But can you prototype a feeling? Can you create an architecture that will touch the soul of people experiencing it in the way that, for example, Louis Kahn's Salk Institute in La Jolla, California, touched the souls of practice principals Ma Yansong and Dang Qun when they visited it, not through the qualities of its concrete or execution, but in standing between the buildings and looking out at the ocean? Can you prototype the ineffable?

MAD's working methods are unique. In the early stages of each project, an artist or sculptor acts as a mentor and questions the architects in order to draw out the feeling they are searching for. Sitting on Dang's desk is a model that has undergone several revisions as she and Ma consider whether it is successfully conveying what they want. At first it was concrete and solid glass; later, green landscape was added. Ma, however, still felt that it failed to capture what was in his mind. They tried adding water and a garden with living plants, which they watered every day. The water, they found, reflected the building.

The Hutong Bubble (2008–9) is a sort of built idea, a pure feeling. The structure itself was designed to 'disappear' and leave only a reflection

1–2. Hutong Bubble, Beijing, China, 2008–9: A computer rendering of a Hutong Bubble seen at street level (top), and a physical scale model of Hutong Bubbles in a Beijing neighbourhood.

3 (opposite). A partial view of the built Hutong Bubble, with the rooftops of the surrounding houses in the foreground.

4

6

5

4. Hutong Bubble: Fabrication of the internal metal frame.

5. The structure's reflective properties 'morph' the surrounding buildings and landscape, while also realizing the architect's intentions of giving the structure the appearance of an alien.

6. The structure's rooftop exit, displaying the effect of the reflective metal cladding.

7–8. Harbin Cultural Center, Heilongjiang, China, 2015: Actual-size mock-ups of the tessellated glazing and cladding (top); the building under construction, showing the complexity of the steel framing used for the roof.

of the historic urban fabric and trees surrounding it. At the same time it has a unique presence intended to contribute to the reinvigoration of the historic *hutongs* (narrow streets or alleys) of Beijing, going beyond restoration or imitation. One might call it a prototype, but Dang does not give it that name. It is made of 2-millimetre-thick sheet steel, welded to a hollow steel frame and chromed off-site to give it its highly polished exterior. Certainly, the built example is a prototype for a vision of much wider deployment contributing to the character of an entire area.

In 2010 MAD won the competition to design a cultural centre for Harbin Cultural Island, a devolpment located in the wetlands to the north of Songhua River in north-east China. Completed in 2015, the Harbin Cultural Center is clad in custom-made white aluminium, in order to be one with the snow-covered landscape in which it sits. White stone and concrete have also been used. Full-scale façade mock-ups played an important role in the development of the building.

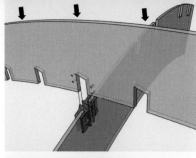

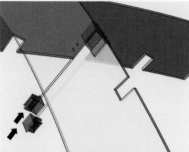

1–3

3·14

Nex— [Alan Dempsey]

A prototype is something conceived to evolve a project, not completely transform it

Alan Dempsey, director of London-based practice Nex—, believes that architectural prototypes can be defined in two different yet related ways. First, they are essentially abstract concepts that can be used to explore fairly precise relationships within a given project. Secondly, they have the capacity to instrumentalize decisions within projects targeting specific outcomes. Seen this way, he argues, their inherently abstract nature allows them to be re-contextualized for entirely different projects, rather than perform a one-off role within a single project.

The prototype for the DRL10 Pavilion at London's Architectural Association (AA) illustrates this potential versatility. It was the first outing for what the practice describes as a 'deep surface'. In the context of the pavilion itself, erected in 2008 to celebrate ten years of the AA's Design Research Laboratory, the deep surface formed both the pavilion's shape and its structure. The deep-surface system was later used for the restoration of an eighteenth-century building, a process in which it evolved from being a building itself – the AA pavilion – into a 30-metre-long, environmentally high-performance roof. As a double-skinned, deep-truss system, it was designed to help regulate the building's internal environment by controlling solar gain on the outside while letting in judicious amounts of sunlight. At the same time, the internal surface was made semi-permeable, creating a 'translucent' air-conditioning system.

In migrating prototypes from project to project, just as their individual qualities have the potential to change considerably between

1–3. DRL10 Pavilion, Architectural Association, London, UK, 2008: Details of joint components and assembly.

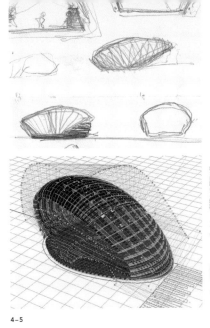

4-5

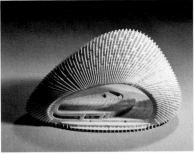

6-7

8

projects, so too can their scale. Another of the practice's deep-surface projects – the Powerscourt Town Centre in Dublin – involved placing a new roof over a large courtyard. Again, this was a highly sophisticated roof structure with excellent environmental credentials. A scaled prototype of its reciprocating timber-lattice form was later transformed into a furniture project: the 'To & Fro Table' (2010). Obviously, the table, some 4,000 per cent smaller than the courtyard roof, performed an entirely different function from that of its antecedent. Composed of a delicate set of timber fins, the lattice tabletop was designed in such a way that its transparency varies depending on the angle from which it is viewed. A person sitting opposite you might have a partial view of your legs, for example, while someone sitting further along the table would be able to see only your top half.

For a practice that has developed the idea of the 'resilient prototype', there are no hard-and-fast rules about scale. Nex— has embraced the notion of the 'working prototype', which does not have to be 1:1 but nevertheless has to offer performance that can be measured and scaled up to correlate directly with the intended in-use performance of the design at full size. In Dempsey's experience, the prototype has been far more useful as a key part of the early stages of design than simply as a means of fine-tuning the design towards the end of the process. He alludes to the automotive and aeronautical industries, in which projects can be digitally prototyped right through

4-5. DRL10 Pavilion: Early concept sketches and digital production model.

6-7. 1:10-scale component prototyping and a physical model of the pavilion.

8. The interior of the completed pavilion.

10–11

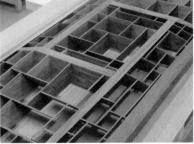

12–13

14–15

to the production of the first working vehicle. The one-off nature of the construction industry, where 'every building is a prototype', is partly the reason he believes that architectural practice still leans towards conventional design approaches. Prototypes are expensive, especially if what they set out to prove merely proves them to be unviable. If anything, he believes that architects are now less likely to experiment with the gusto and optimism of, say, the Eameses or Alison and Peter Smithson, owing to a combination of tighter legal and health-and-safety constraints and their direct affect on costs. He does, however, cite some notable exceptions: SHoP Architects in New York (see page 146), Helen & Hard in Stavanger, Ball-Nogues Studio in Los Angeles. Clearly, Nex— should be included in this list.

9 (opposite). DRL10 Pavilion: The completed pavilion on Bedord Square, London.

10–11. 'To & Fro Table', London, 2010: Early prototypes of table joints, seen individually and part-assembled.

12–13. Views of the top and underside of the first prototype table.

14–15. The completed prototype table.

1–2

3·15

EMBT [Benedetta Tagliabue]

A step in the process of transformation

Italian architect Benedetta Tagliabue notes that, in contrast to the architectural model, which helps the client understand a project, the prototype is mainly something for the architect. It is a step in the process of transforming a design little by little, to ensure that everything is working. It should also be something you have not seen before, otherwise why do it? For the complex geometries that characterize EMBT's work, the prototype reveals the things that the architects had never thought about, even when, in the digital drawings and models, everything seems just so. The practice remains craft-based, cautious about handing over to a CNC technician in a model shop. In particular, it is wary of the potential laziness that creeps in by going totally digital and 'letting the machine do it'. When it comes to checking and understanding a design in-depth, the handmade process has some distinct advantages.

For the new Scottish Parliament building in Edinburgh (2004), the practice had the option of using full-scale prototypes, such as a 1:1 prototype of part of the façade. It was very expensive, however, with all the final textures and finishes, and probably came too early in the process, particularly in such a contractually complex project with so many elements going to different contractors. The most useful prototypes, the practice found, were at 1:5 scale. These were development prototypes that the construction company could then develop to determine detail, fabrication workflow, mechanization and so on. Although detailed, such prototypes allow room for further detail and development.

1–2. Scottish Parliament, Edinburgh, Scotland, 2004: Two views of the physical model.

3 (opposite). Spanish Pavilion, Expo 2010, Shanghai, China: Working models being made at EMBT in March 2010.

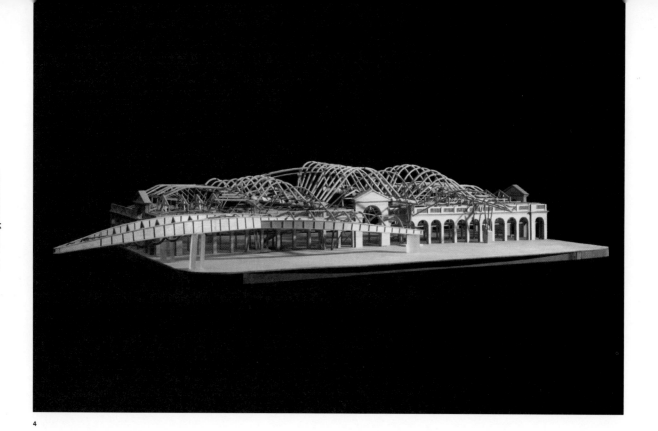

4

4. Santa Caterina Market, Barcelona, Spain, 2005: A model of the market showing the framework for the roof. The pergola in the foreground was not built.

The roof for the Santa Caterina Market in Barcelona (2005) was totally experimental and unique. It required a great deal of prototyping in the office, including 1:5 experimental models to see if the wood could be bent into the desired shape. This in turn required close collaboration with the structural engineer and the fabrication company, in order to be confident that the performance of the models would translate to full scale.

For the Spanish Pavilion at Expo 2010 in Shanghai, there was no time or money to produce a full-scale prototype or mock-up of the entire façade. Rather, EMBT made numerous full-scale prototypes of the individual panels, as well as 1:20 models, together with digital renders and models of the way they would come together. There was a great deal of anxiety in the practice about what the façade would look like, and how it would function. In the end, the design worked as planned, although there was a sense that the absence of a full-scale prototype had generated excessive risk.

The realization of full-scale prototypes involves clients not only recognizing the complexities of the design and the importance of the prototype as a way to mitigate risk and cost, but also being prepared to finance the cost. It then requires specialist skills, know-how and experience to design and produce a high-quality yet affordable prototype capable of displaying all the characteristics and functionality of the built design. This expertise, whether in the form of a specialist consultant or manufacturer, is not available everywhere, and is highly dependent for its survival on favourable macroeconomics in the local area.

5–6

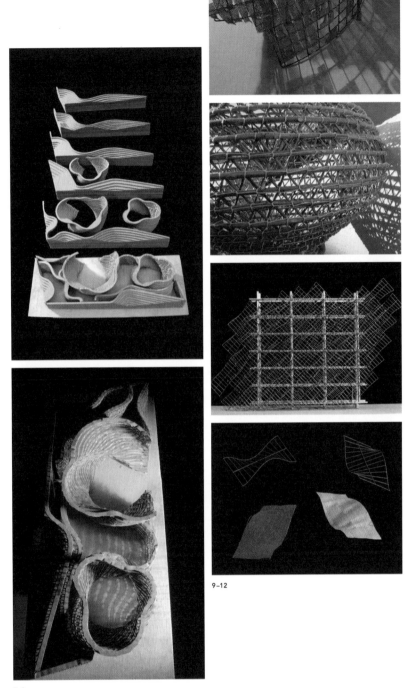

7–8

9–12

5–12. Spanish Pavilion: Façade studies
with Chinese characters in 3D (fig. 5)
and interior view, competition panel,
2007 (fig. 6); cardboard working models,
October 2007 (figs 7–8); wicker panel
and weaving tests (figs 9–10); a working
1:25 model and studio weaving tests
(figs 11–12).

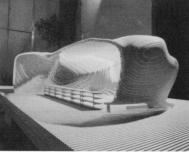

1–3

3·16

dECOi architects [Mark Goulthorpe]

Prototyping towards the archetype

According to Mark Goulthorpe, principal at dECOi architects and an associate professor in the Department of Architecture at MIT, prototyping ensures that, to some degree, invention displaces reliance on expertise – in other words, that there is a different set of drivers behind cultural production beyond the emulation of prior excellence. Indeed, for Goulthorpe, it is this drive towards novelty and innovation that makes design so compelling. Moreover, he believes that, in terms of validating a process, the ultimate prototype is the completed building, an archetype for future aspirations.

For Goulthorpe, a model is a formal representation of intentions, whereas a prototype is for testing something, usually technical, along the way. He describes mock-ups as tools for 'relaxing' the client, having found that, for such projects as One Main in Boston (2008–9), describing the prototype as a mock-up made the client much more comfortable with the design process. It seems, therefore, that definitions depend on the message the architect wants to be received. He recalls Professor Frédéric Migayrou (Bartlett School of Architecture and Centre Pompidou) entering dECOi's ¼-scale 'version' of its proposed Minan Gallery in Paris and exclaiming that this was not a model but a 'small version of the real thing'.

In terms of dECOi's approach to design, this is an apt observation. In practice, dECOi skates around the complicated model/mock-up/prototype distinction through Goulthorpe's prescient grasp of the fact that, in the world of digital fabrication, achieving an outcome goes

1–3. Miran Gallery, Paris, France, 2003: Quarter-scale prototype of the timber interior.

4–5

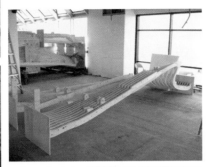

6–7

8

4–5. One Main, Boston, MA, 2008–9: The reception desk undergoes CNC milling and pre-assembly at the workshop of the engineering and fabrication company CW Keller.

6–7. A pre-assembled ceiling component prior to installation.

8. A view of the completed interior.

hand in hand with designing the outcome itself. The same production protocols are used for the scaled prototype as for the completed artefact. In the case of the HypoSurface, early scaled-down versions were powered with smaller versions of the pistons to be used at full scale.

In Goulthorpe's experience, providing clients with a working prototype has been essential to gaining their trust. It is all very well testing performance, he says, but the bigger test is attaining client confidence and, ultimately, their approval. As for the role of the virtual prototype, Goulthorpe is convinced that architects are still a considerable distance from where they need to be. He cites numerous examples from parallel professions of just how much can be simulated virtually with absolute confidence, rendering physical prototyping technically unnecessary. That said, and despite his access to the latest technology at MIT, he retains a strong belief in the power of physical prototypes.

When it comes to encouraging clients to invest directly in prototyping, Goulthorpe takes a unique approach. Rather than positioning the prototype as an experiment, which clients may be unwilling to pay for, he positions it as a proof of concept. Crucially, such an approach is backed up by a novel fee structure, where the client is billed on the basis of being provided with a successful prototype. In addition to demonstrating the courage of Goulthorpe's convictions, it is proof of the practice's ongoing commitment to seeing the built design as a prototype along a journey that continues beyond the individual project.

Design is all about exploration and the creation of something new. Thus, for many of the leading innovators in architecture and building design engaged in conversation for this book, each of their projects is a prototype in its own right. But if every project they work on does not reach this status, then the prized ones certainly do – they are one of a kind, the first of their ilk, leading to broader innovation.

Norwegian practice Snøhetta speaks of projects that are forms of research, extraordinary in nature, and which do something very different. This implies the use of new processes and approaches to design as much as it does novelty in the outcomes. The whole project – its design, its realization, its lifecycle – is an experimental prototype. For Blumer-Lehmann of Switzerland, all its non-standard projects are sites for the development of new processes in order to realize those projects; seen another way, projects are prototypes for testing new design and production methods. Frankfurt-based Bollinger + Grohmann only takes on projects that are prototypes, the first of a kind, and believes that the only real testing of a prototype occurs on-site during and following construction of the actual building.

The first, or 'proto', in these instances refers to the whole, as does the 'type'; each is not only one of a kind but also, more crucially, the first of its kind, an archetype from which imitations or copies of the whole or part may follow, but only on completion of the project or building, and only from the ateliers of others. By then, these designers of prototypes will have moved on to something new.

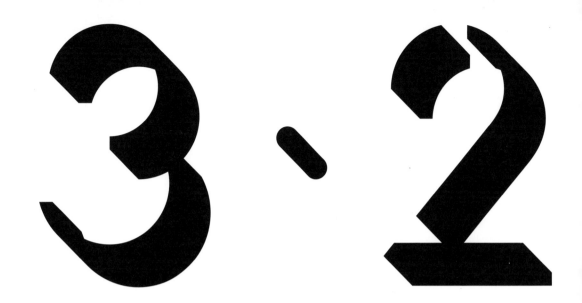

3.2

The Project as Prototype

1–2

3·21

Snøhetta

The project is the prototype

Based in Oslo, Snøhetta is an international practice specializing not only in architecture but also in landscape, interior and brand design. It routinely builds full-scale prototypes for its projects, as well as working at other scales, and possesses well-equipped handwork, CNC and robotic workshops for this purpose. When the occasion demands it, such as in the case of outdoor lighting, which can never be fully simulated in a darkroom environment, it also creates prototypes 'live' on-site. The practice is led by a mantra of 'instant prototyping' for all types of design work, and at all stages of the design process: the beginning, the middle and the end.

According to Snøhetta, however, the real prototypes are the singular projects that test something genuinely new. Asked to provide three exemplars of such prototypes – 'game changers' that break with tradition – the practice selected the King Abdulaziz Centre for World Culture (completion due 2016), 'A House to Die In' (a collaboration with the artist Bjarne Melgaard; 2011–) and MAX IV (2016).

King Abdulaziz Centre for World Culture

Located in Dhahran, a city in the Eastern Province of Saudi Arabia, the King Abdulaziz Centre for World Culture is a large-scale, competition-winning architectural and landscape project for the Saudi Aramco oil company. The centre is intended to promote cultural development within Saudi Arabia, and includes a 930-seat auditorium, a cinema, an exhibition

1–2. King Abdulaziz Centre for World Culture, Dhahran, Saudi Arabia, 2007–16: Façade details.

3 (opposite). A full-scale mock-up of a façade detail is tested on-site for the affects of weather.

4–5

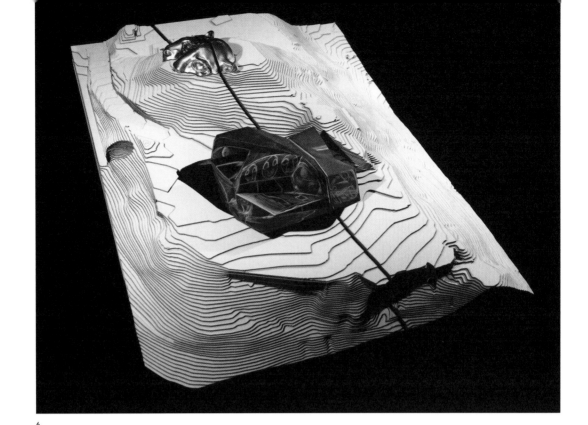

6

hall, a museum, a library and an archive. The concept behind the centre's striking, futuristic design is 'pebbles landing in a desert landscape'. Among its many unusual design features is a unique and highly complex façade system, which is being manufactured in the semi-arid lowlands of Saudi Arabia itself. The design of the façade involved extensive prototyping and the creation of numerous mock-ups. Given the harsh conditions of the desert environment in which the centre is located, it was particularly important to ensure that the façade would not become clogged up with sand. Other factors that were subject to testing included durability and ease of maintenance

'A House to Die In'

The aim of this ongoing project – a collaboration with Norwegian artist Bjarne Melgaard, commissioned by the Selvaag family and Sealbay AS – is to realize a house for the artist to live and work in. The challenge of maintaining the inherent quality and identity of Melgaard's work encouraged Snøhetta to depart from the comfort of familiar creative processes. While the practice's concerns remain architectural, Melgaard is fearful of inhabiting a world of pure architecture.

'In this project,' explained Snøhetta co-founder Kjetil Thorsen, 'the joint authorship reflects the complexity of [Melgaard's] artwork. Working with Bjarne challenges us to discover the boundaries of our capabilities.'

4–5. King Abdulaziz Centre for World Culture: The project was modelled on the concept of pebbles in the desert sand.

6. 'A House to Die In', Oslo, Norway, 2011–: A topographical model showing the proposed location of the house.

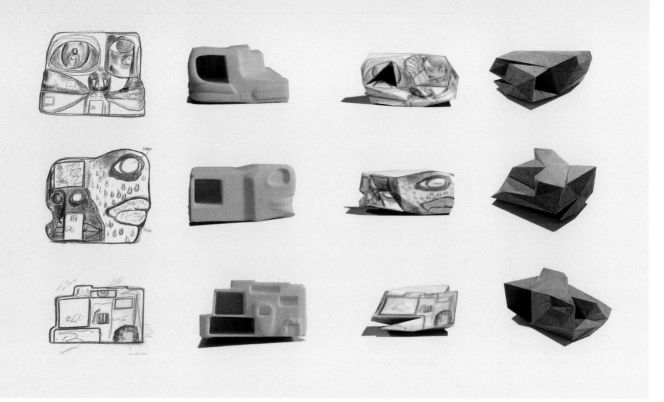

7

7. 'A House to Die In': An illustration showing the process of transforming artist Bjarne Melgaard's sketches into 3D architectonic volumes.

Both sides have been challenged, with Snøhetta prototyping ways to interpret Melgaard's 2D and analogue drawings as 3D digital renderings and objects. There have been multiple stages of re-representation, using a variety of mathematical abstraction processes, in order to distill Melgaard's thought-provoking concept and vision of a house 'to die in'.

MAX IV

Whether directly or indirectly, clients have to pay for prototyping. Significantly, however, the process has the potential to save many times its cost. A case in point is the landscaping project undertaken by Snøhetta at MAX IV, a state-of-the-art synchrotron radiation facility at the University of Lund in southern Sweden, part of the city of Lund's new science and innovation campus. Snøhetta was engaged to provide a landscape design for the grounds of the facility.

While the waveform-like design devised by the practice provides an obvious conceptual link to the work going on inside MAX IV, it is intended to serve a more practical purpose. Part of the brief was to minimize the vibrations from the adjacent motorway, in order to ensure the proper operation of the facility, especially its subterranean particle accelerator. One way to counter or cancel the vibrations was to introduce greater topographical variety into the surrounding landscape.

8–10

11–12

13–14

8–10. MAX IV, Lund, Sweden, 2011–16: A sequence of illustrations showing how the landscape's dynamic design was created. The design is intended to minimize the effect of vibrations from a nearby motorway.

11–12. An artist's impresssion of the completed landscape.

13–14. Aerial photographs showing the landscape under construction. Such photographs were taken on a monthly basis.

Using the wavelengths of the vibrations experienced by the site as its starting point, Snøhetta generated a variety of landscape designs consisting of intersecting 'ripples'.

Digital prototyping was used to ensure that the finished design could be achieved using the existing volume of ground mass, meaning that nothing had to be transported either off or on to the site. The design also had to be capable of managing storm-water run-off, including the large amounts of water delivered by extreme weather events, while remaining stable at all times.

The principal means of communication between the architects, the clients, the consultants and the contractors were 1:2,000 rapid prototypes of the landscape designs. Produced directly from digital 3D models created using Rhino 3D modelling software, these prototypes were critical to a sound, shared understanding of the huge amounts of earth that needed to be moved, and hence to the quick completion of the design-development stage. The digital 3D models were later translated into GPS coordinates for use by the bulldozer operators.

The excavations began in 2011, and 70 per cent of the landscaping had been completed by the time construction of the facility itself had begun. When the building opens, meadow grass and harvestable plants – selected in consultation with specialists at the Swedish University of Agricultural Sciences in Alnarp – will have already had three seasons' worth of growth on the new slopes.

1–3

← Techniques
2.2 / p. 27 / Mock-ups
2.4 / p. 37 / CNC Revolution
2.5 / p. 41 / Prototyping Through Subtraction

Blumer-Lehmann

Project as prototype: prototyping processes

The Swiss company Blumer-Lehmann describes itself as a pioneer in innovative timber construction and sustainability, closing the circle between creative production and all areas – economical and ecological – of the timber supply chain. Half of the work it is engaged in is non-standard, and rather than compete with local firms engaged in standard work, it chooses to collaborate with them. Blumer-Lehmann has been involved in the design and execution of some of the most exacting, complex timber architecture in the world. For the firm's Martin Antemann, everything it does is a prototype. Each project is unique and requires the development of a unique process. Everything is done for the first time: the project is the prototype.

Full-scale mock-ups are a critical part of the process, preferably constructed very early on – either at or before the tender stage, and certainly before committing to sourcing large quantities of material, at which point the cost of change becomes prohibitive. You cannot scale up the grain of timber or its structural performance, so working at full scale and building close facsimiles is essential to evaluating such aspects of a project as its feasibility, tolerances and sequence of construction, as well as the overlaps between the different parties involved. While sophisticated digital modelling and automated fabrication workflows are key to both Blumer-Lehmann's communication with others and its own processes, the company has no intention of replacing full-scale mock-ups with virtual representation. In fact, it has become more usual for clients

1–3. Kilden Performing Arts Centre, Kristiansand, Norway, 2012: Mock-ups of the roofing system.

4–6

7

8

4–6. Tamedia Office Building, Zurich, Switzerland, 2013: Full-scale mock-ups.

7. A view through the structure of the building at lounge level.

8. The building under construction.

to receive physical samples or mock-ups as part of the building-tender process or the pre-qualification of tenderers. However, the building needs to be especially complex for the contractor to request or fund prototypes.

Although each of the company's projects is unique, its approach to prototyping is in some ways more industrial than architectural, owing mainly to the scale of production. For the Kilden Performing Arts Centre in Kristiansand, Norway, designed by Finnish architects ALA in collaboration with SMS Arkitekter AS, and built with the detailed design input of designtoproduction, some 1,700 unique beams had to be prototyped. In the case of Shigeru Ban's Tamedia Office Building in Zurich, a total of 3,500 component assemblies were required.

Physical samples and mock-ups are important for testing aesthetics, leading either to the commitment of the client and architect or to a change in the design. Such samples are equally important for performance testing. For the Tamedia Office Building, for example, a structural 'net' of beams was sent to the laboratory and tested to destruction. On more than one occasion, Antemann himself has taken samples home as part of the testing process. During one project, no one could or would provide a specification for the gluing of several thousand joints. Taking the samples back to his house, Antemann ensured that the moisture content was correct before gluing and clamping them for thirty minutes. The samples were then tested in Blumer-Lehmann's structure lab so that the company could provide a guaranteed specification itself.

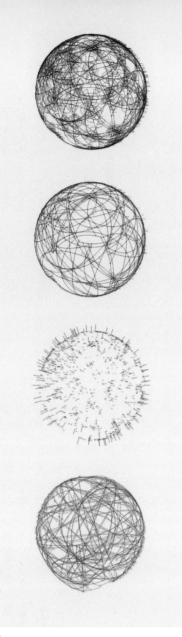

1

1. 'Sphere', Deutsche Bank, Frankfurt, Germany, 2011 (Mario Bellini Architects): Modelling software was used to determine the optimum structure of the sphere. The completed sphere hangs in the entrance hall of Deutsche Bank's offices in Frankfurt.

3 · 23

← Techniques
2.5 / p. 41 / Prototyping Through Subtraction
2.6 / p. 45 / Prototyping Through Addition
2.8 / p. 53 / Virtual Prototyping

Bollinger + Grohmann

[Manfred Grohmann / Marc Fahlbusch / Kim Boris Löffler]

Every building is a prototype

Manfred Grohmann, Marc Fahlbusch and Kim Boris Löffler all agree that every building Bollinger + Grohmann (B+G) is involved with is, in itself, a prototype. With each new project, the company attempts something new and unique. Others may adopt the novel idea from an existing project and use it in their own work, but B+G sets out to do something different every time. Thus, it views each building as a prototype for the world of design and construction, rather than a serial prototype in the development of its own *oeuvre*. Moreover, it believes that if a prototype is a way to test a design, technically, then the real testing happens on-site, during the construction of the building at full scale. The European Central Bank in Frankfurt (2014) – for which B+G acted as structural engineer – is a good example of this approach. In the initial design, the diagonals connecting the building's two slender towers were positioned at random; later, their location was optimized and reorganized through a digital process. But there are also huge items embedded in the concrete, and whether everything would work together as planned did not become apparent until the engineers were on-site to find out.

While a model does not have to be completely true to the finished article, a prototype – the purpose of which is to develop and test new ideas – needs to have much more in common with the design as built. In this respect, such forms of rapid prototyping as 3D printing currently fall short of their name in one important respect: material veracity. Structural engineers, for example, cannot really check the structural properties of

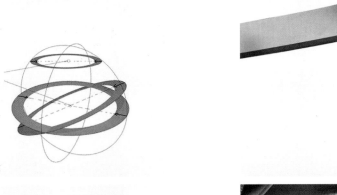

2–4

5–6

2–4. 'Sphere': Generating geometry
to construct the sphere.

5–6. Mock-up at the Arnold AG,
inspecting the precision.

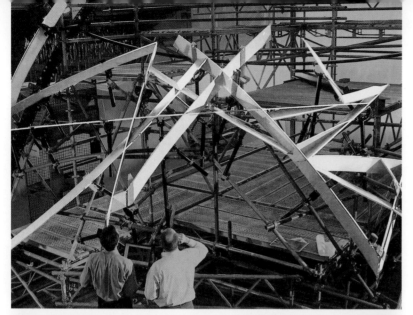

9–11

7–8

7–8. 'Sphere': The mock-up under construction at the German metal-working company Arnold AG.

9–11. The completed structure, as seen from different viewpoints inside the bank.

12–13

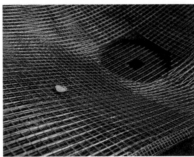

14–15

16–17

12–15. 'Parapluie', prototype bus-stop shelter, Frankfurt, Germany, 2013 (schneider+schumacher): Manufacturing the formwork for the concrete canopy.

16–17. Assembly and load-testing of the canopy.

a design unless they are working with the real materials. If it were possible to print accurately in concrete and steel, rapid prototyping would be extremely important. As it is, the next best form of prototyping for testing performance, after the construction of the building itself, is digital 3D modelling, which allows for testing through analysis and calculation.

In terms of prototyping individual building elements so that they can be tested prior to construction, glass roofs have to be designed to withstand objects being thrown on them; indeed, some buildings need to be bombproof. While clients are sometimes willing to pay for façade prototypes that can be tested in a wind tunnel, they generally pay for looks rather than technical detail, and there is a great deal more 3D modelling and rapid prototyping for shared understanding and communication than in the past. In the digital century, the design process is becoming much more varied. Consider, for example, the process used by Peter Cook for the Kunsthaus Graz (completed 2003). While Cook started with a physical model of the building, which became the basis for the digital 3D modelling that followed, it is now common to start by modelling with a computer and printing physical 3D models as visual proofs of concept along the way.

As Fahlbusch notes, thirty years ago an architect or draftsperson would spend a great deal of time thinking about a design before committing anything to paper. Today, designers can simply jump straight in because they can throw a design away and print another one in a couple of hours. This tests ideas but not whether they work.

1–3

← Techniques
2.3 / p. 31 / Prototyping Performance
2.5 / p. 41 / Prototyping Through Subtraction
2.8 / p. 53 / Virtual Prototyping

Cloud 9 Architects [Enric Ruiz-Geli]

A prototype is something between a patent and the user

Every project undertaken by Cloud 9 is described by the Spanish practice as being a 'pilot project': it is always unique. In what comes across as a rather esoteric definition, Enric Ruiz-Geli proposes that a prototype 'is something between a patent and the user'. Cloud 9's goal is to make invention and innovation the signature of its design approach, patenting technical discoveries along the way. Prototyping is therefore a testing activity for the practice, especially in the case of a newly invented device that may help to boost a building's performance, giving the building's user a boost too. Take any of the practice's projects – be it the Media-TIC building in Barcelona, Villa Nurbs in Empuriabrava or the recently completed Case Study House in Begur, and it is very clear that Cloud 9's aim is to change substantially the construction, performance and look of contemporary architecture.

Ruiz-Geli distinguishes between models and prototypes by attributing to each of them different communication tasks. Models, he believes, are a means of visually communicating concepts among the design team, whereas prototypes are for communicating performance, as well as helping to envisage and test new ideas. For Cloud 9, an architectural practice driven by the act of making, the prototype has a fundamental role in testing performance. Given that each of the practice's projects has performance as its key design driver, this is not surprising.

But isn't this an absolutist stance? Most probably, yes, especially in light of the fact that Ruiz-Geli rejects any potential role for mock-ups.

1–3. Case Study House, Aigua Blava, Begur, Spain, 2015: Exterior and interior views of the completed building.

4

5–6

7–8

4–8. Case Study House: Prefabricated coffered permanent formwork for the wall-roof construction. The interior surface is tiled, while the coffers receive insulation and a fibre-reinforced concrete substrate for the exterior tiling.

Indeed, he considers mock-ups as keeping the designer from having a meaningful dialogue with the process of designing-through-making, and the making of prototypes in particular. In effect, his studio just prototypes, eschewing both modelling and mock-ups as part of the design process: to Cloud 9, modelling and mock-ups *represent* design, rather than push it. The practice prototypes at a small scale during a project's initial stages, moving on to larger prototypes once it has partnered with the fabricators and builders with which it will develop the project, and eventually using on-site prototypes. It considers the final prototype in this process as being the completed building.

Ruiz-Geli is adamant that as useful as digital prototyping is to the office, it does not offer the same benefits as physical prototyping; and certainly, it is ascribed a subservient role within the practice. He appreciates the relative speed with which virtual tests – such as the simulation of fluxes and flows, particle systems and defined behaviours – can be prepared and run, but these are considered only steps along the way to realizing the physical prototype, always the 'real prototype'.

As for who pays for the prototyping at Cloud 9, there are no hard and fast rules. Ruiz-Geli characterizes his practice as design research aligned to industrial research, in terms of experimentation, development through learning and, ultimately, patenting. In some cases, where the intellectual property is being shared, the client will co-invest in the research, taking a share of the value of any invention beyond the actual building they

9

11–12

10

9–12. Pavilion 3 at the Case Study House, made by students from Art Center College of Design, Pasadena, CA, in collaboration with Cloud 9 Architects: An inflated, ellipsoid bladder receives a double-membrane skin with a pattern of plywood shapes acting as clamps. A fibre-reinforced concrete slurry was gravity-fed between the double membranes once they had been draped over the ellipsoid bladder. The slurry invades the spaces between the plywood clamps and forms the network of structural ribs.

originally commissioned. In other cases, the practice shoulders the costs, through a combination of fees and separate financing. Ultimately, the client has come to Cloud 9 for the way in which it carries out its practice. For all his ambition, Ruiz-Geli is realistic about what can be achieved. In the case of Media-TIC, for example, only 15 per cent of the building meets his 'building as prototype' definition; with such large projects as these, he prefers partially to insulate all concerned against the effects of over-complication. For the urban-scale project, the practice therefore employs conventional building systems and materials where appropriate, experimenting only in the areas of most need. With Media-TIC, this was in the area of its environmental performance.

As one might expect in the case of a practice like Cloud 9, driven as it is by inventing, making and testing via the evolving prototype, its buildings are never just a pavilion, a case study, a prototype or even a 'really nice sculpture': they are all of them.

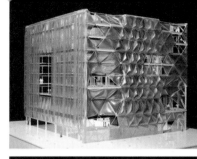

13–14

15–17

18–21

13–14. Media-TIC building, Barcelona, Spain, 2011: Physical and virtual prototypes.

15–17. The building has a giant portal-frame structure, with the services intergrated within the frame. The top of the building was constructed first, and sequentially jacked up to receive each of the lower floors, all of which are suspended from the portal frame (with the exception of the ground floor).

18–21. The building's exterior surfaces feature a variety of innovative energy-management systems, including inflated 'pillows' that can adapt internally to varying amounts of direct sunlight.

1–2

1–2. Pacific Place, Queensway, Hong Kong, 2011: Sand-cast bronze elevator buttons.

3–4. The ribboned steel roof of the café-restaurant at Pacific Place. The roof was made in a Chinese shipyard.

3·25

← Techniques
2.1 / p. 23 / Traditional Techniques
2.2 / p. 27 / Mock-ups

Thomas Heatherwick

Prototyping design in the studio is through hands-on 'making'

For Thomas Heatherwick, prototyping means engaging with real materials and real techniques at full scale. The placing of 'making' at the heart of the design process has been a consistent feature of his practice since the early 1990s, when he was an undergraduate at Manchester Polytechnic studying 3D design, culminating in the building of a pavilion. At that time, physical prototyping was central to the teaching of architecture, with an emphasis on experimentation with real materials at full size. Today, however – as Heatherwick notes – hands-on experimentation is having to compete with students' predilection for increasingly accessible digital fabrication technologies. The fact that Heatherwick can turn his hand to crafts as varied as cabinetmaking, welding, glass-blowing, jewelry and basket-weaving is testament to an absolute personal belief that such skills are fundamental to a designer like himself, nimbly working across the domains of sculptor, architect, engineer, urban designer and product designer. This emphasis on 'making' places Heatherwick firmly in the camp of fully committed *Homo faber*.

In the Heatherwick Studio, prototyping is seen as central to the process of translating ideas into reality. There is an appreciation, too, that until it has proved itself to be a working version of the built design, the prototype is also a test of a project's viability. This holds true whether the object being prototyped is as small as a business card or as large as an advanced building façade costing hundreds of thousands of pounds to prototype. Prototypes are used extensively in the studio to grapple

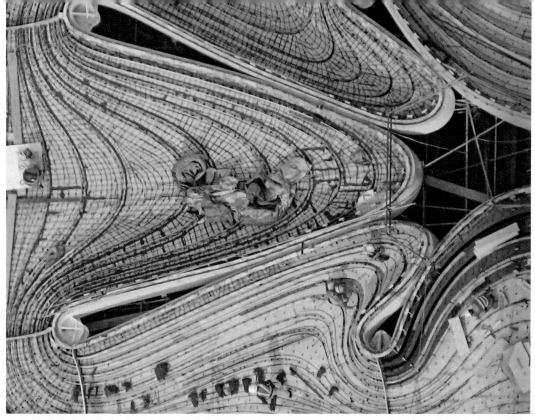

5

5. Designed at Heatherwick Studio, this machine gives 1-millimetre-thick sheets of stainless steel a crumpled texture.

6–7. Aberystwyth Artists' Studios, Wales, 2008: Crumpled-steel cladding.

with the specifics of translating the ideas first manifested in drawings and models into a working version of reality. This pathway to exceptional design includes prototyping the techniques and processes that will be required when making the final product or building.

Given the range of the studio's output and the sheer inventiveness that accompanies every project that emerges from it, regardless of scale or budget, such experimentation and in-use trialling is vital to achieving the early vision that has excited the client into commissioning the studio in the first place. This excitement has to be matched by absolute certainty that the design can leave the studio and exist as a viable, long-term manufactured or built proposition capable of meeting the expectations of the project's commissioner and builder alike. For that reason, the more unusual the proposal, the more committed is the testing of the idea in the studio. Driven by the trust of enlightened clients, projects like Pacific Place in Hong Kong (2011) – where everything is bespoke, from the façade to the elevator buttons – give rise to such innovations as wooden toilet-cubicle doors that do not have hinges, relying instead on repeat bending. In the case of these projects, the studio adopts the component manufacturers' approach to lifecycle testing by building rigs in-house that push such novelty prototypes to their limits, ensuring confidence for all in the ideas that are developed in the studio.

With a working style that is utterly dependent on hands-on making, and as useful as digital design and manufacturing might be in ultimately

11

8

9–10

realizing projects, neither digital technology plays any role in the studio's idea creation and concept development. By contrast, and relying on intense observation and memory, lessons learnt by Heatherwick – even those from student days – are retained by him as potential design opportunities. Seeing aluminium extrusions emerging with unexpected kinks and twists while visiting the now-defunct Alcan Lynemouth smelter in north-east England, for example, led years later to 'Extrusions' (2009), a series of bold, industrial-scale experiments in extruded aluminium, produced in collaboration with a Chinese metals-forming company. The supreme competence of being able to 'make' as part of designing meant that the studio had the confidence to gather all the capital at its disposal and use the world's largest metals-extrusion machine in a far-off location to squeeze these fascinating prototype benches into existence.

8–11. 'Extrusions', Heatherwick
Studio, London, 2009: Bench formed
by extruding an aluminium ingot through
a die under enormous pressure.

12 (opposite). Middle section of the
extruded bench.

Failure is an inherent part of prototyping. Prototypes are used to fail earlier and faster, to discover the precise mechanisms and modes of failure or the aspects of a design that do not meet expectations. This detailed knowledge of the shortcomings of a design is used to refine a proposal and move forward. It may also be used to come up with a new design altogether.

While the practices discussed in the previous section adhere to the idea of the project as prototype, subjected as it is to the ultimate test of success during construction, the emphasis in the conversations distilled in this section is on early and appropriate testing of design hypotheses. The appropriateness of a test may depend on the scale of the model or prototype. Material behaviour, such as elasticity, or grain direction in timber, for example, might only be meaningfully exhibited through full-scale physical testing. Appropriateness may also rest on the availability and affordability of materials or fabrication techniques, or on time frames in the building schedule. Apposite testing might also hinge on budgetary considerations that can only be revealed through a prototype of the proposal as a highly detailed cost estimate.

Prototypes of cost, materiality or the complex or novel parts of a design, including their assembly, may be motivated as much by the need to verify a hypothesis as by the need to seek its falsification or failure. In this sense, for the client commissioning the design of something totally new, prototyping is a risk-mitigation strategy, a means of confirming that the design can indeed be built and will be aesthetically successful – or even that it will provide appropriate fire-resistance.

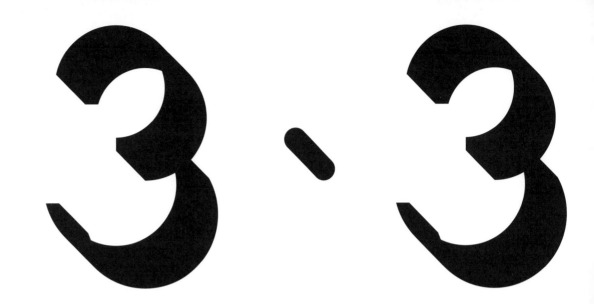

Experimental Verification / Falsification

1–3

← Techniques
2.2 / p. 27 / Mock-ups
2.3 / p. 31 / Prototyping Performance
2.5 / p. 41 / Prototyping Through Subtraction

designtoproduction

Prototype as experiment to test / falsify

1–3. Kilden Performing Arts Centre, Kristiansand, Norway, 2012: A selection of the CNC-machined timber components used for the façade.

4–6. The curved beams were cut so as to enable the precise positioning of the cladding strips over the difficult geometrical terrain of the façade, accomplishing an even aesthetic without awkward angles between the strips.

7–8. A mock-up of a single façade element. Following this assembly test at the Swiss timber contractor, the parts were shipped to Norway and the full mock-up was assembled.

The Zurich-based company designtoproduction is a leader in 'realizing complexity in architecture', serving as a consultancy for the digital production of complex designs. For founding partner Fabian Scheurer, a prototype – like a scientific experiment – cannot establish truth or efficacy, but is a means of falsifying something. To that end, it must be as close to the 'real thing' as possible, in a way that allows something specific to be tested. The company spends only 15 per cent of its time working with designers; the rest it devotes to the 'back end', developing the systems that allow complex designs to be realized by fabricators and contractors. The information it provides others allows them to build physical prototypes for testing a design and, ultimately, to digitally fabricate and construct it.

For the Kilden Performing Arts Centre in Kristiansand, Norway, designtoproduction was tasked by the Norwegian timber contractor Trebyggeriet with finding a way to create a 3,500-square-metre oak-covered façade. This dramatic architectural element traces the profiles of the centre's multiple auditoria in a sweeping, undulating surface that rises from the base of the lobby to the straight edge of the external cantilevered roof. Resolving the freeform geometry into a finely detailed and apparently simple surface of oak strips was a task of the greatest complexity, calling for a combination of geometrical and fabrication gymnastics and a keen understanding of the performance and processing of materials. The complexity and aesthetic uncertainties were such that it also called for the detailed prototyping and mock-up of both the process and the outcome.

4–6

7–8

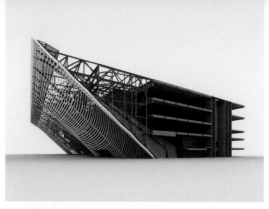

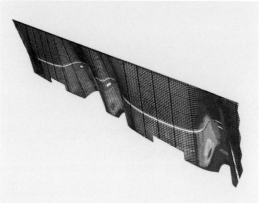

9–10

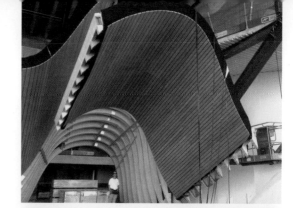

11–12

9. Kilden Performing Arts Centre: Digital model showing how the curved, CNC-cut timber sills are suspended from a red steel structure above.

10. Stress analysis of the timber members. The 'hotspots' reveal areas of stress concentration.

11. Installation of the pre-assembled sections of the façade.

12. The completed façade, as seen from the interior of the building.

13–14. An exterior view and detail of the completed façade.

Before designtoproduction had joined the project, two prototypes had been constructed at half scale. For Scheurer, the failing of these prototypes underlines the importance of fully understanding the issues around scaling and of working at full scale when what you are testing demands it. The early scaled prototypes were made of steel with plywood cladding, but the steel – the key performance factors of which are bendability and spring – could not be bent precisely enough, since such qualities are difficult to test meaningfully except at full scale. When using prototypes as a means of falsification, it is impossible to be certain that something is not performing except by measuring performance that is very close to the real thing. With the Kilden project, prototyping the system using curved, CNC-cut timber instead of steel, and undertaking detailed measurement of the performance, led to a significant change in the construction plan.

Scheurer also works with architecture students to impart an understanding of the demands of building at full scale and the importance of prototyping and testing. He believes that although the trend in architecture schools towards undertaking full-scale fabrication projects is positive, the nettle of assembly has yet to be fully grasped, either by the architectural profession or by the construction industry. It is important, he feels, to prototype the actual assembly process and sequence to avoid the illusion of automation that the use of laser-cutting and 3D printing can induce. After all, you can crash-test a car but never a whole building.

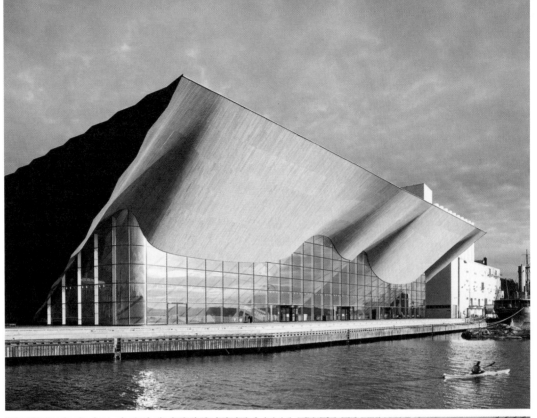

13–14

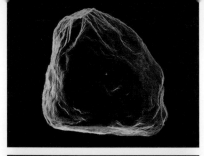

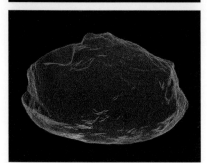

1–4

1–4. *Rock on Top of Another Rock*, Kensington Gardens, London, 2013: Each rock was scanned using 3D terrestrial lidar to generate a set of data points (figs 1 and 3). These were then converted into two highly accurate closed-surface STL (stereolithography) files, one for each rock (figs 2 and 4).

3 · 32

← Techniques
2.3 / p. 31 / Prototyping Performance
2.2 / p. 27 / Mock-ups
2.8 / p. 53 / Virtual Prototyping

Arup [Ed Clark / Alice Blair]

Designing buildings as serial prototypes

Balancing one rock on top of another in London's Kensington Gardens would seem to lack prospects in terms of informing a discussion on prototyping in architecture, but Arup director Ed Clark and senior engineer Alice Blair would have you think otherwise. Clark and Blair were the engineers for the temporary sculpture *Rock on Top of Another Rock*, commissioned by the Serpentine Gallery from the Swiss artist Peter Fischli, and on display from March 2013 to September 2014.

Standing on a concrete base, the 5.5-metre-high sculpture consisted of a 30-tonne granite boulder resting improbably on top of a second boulder of similar dimensions. The care taken by the artists to source from the British countryside suitably ordinary glacial rocks was matched only by the care taken by the engineers to sit one on top of the other, with the lower boulder seeming hardly to touch the ground. Seeing the park as a contrived wilderness, the artists wanted to make the same gesture that many cultures make when marking the land through which they have passed: the placing of one stone on top of another to signal a route back.

The challenge for Clark and Blair was to find a method by which they could balance two irregularly shaped rocks in a safe and stable manner without compromising the artists' vision, and assemble them on-site in a straightforward and uncomplicated way. At the site of the stones' origin, a 3D terrestrial lidar scanner was used to create a set of data points accurate to less than 2 millimetres. The data points were converted into 3D volumes, which, in turn, were used for computational volumetric

5–7

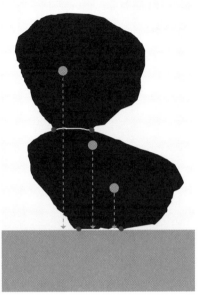

8

9

5–7. *Rock on Top of Another Rock*:
The rocks were scanned at their original
location in North Wales.

8. The STL files were imported into
3D modelling software, providing useful
secondary data, including volume,
surface area and centres of gravity.

9. The assembled sculpture at
Kensington Gardens in London.

analysis and to generate 1:20 3D prints, allowing the boulders' centre of
gravity to be calculated. At the same time, the artists, who were seeking
to achieve the sense of poise that was demanded of one rock balanced
on top of another with no mechanical support or fixing, worked with the
physical scale models.

Close study of the actual rocks revealed fissures that, if one was
placed on top of the other without due consideration, could cause them
to shatter under their own weight. Prototyping using both the digital and
the physical models meant that a solution could be reached that suited
everyone. The sculpture was duly assembled in less than three hours, after
which the rocks were re-scanned in order to confirm that they were in
the correct position. They were also load-tested to ensure that the lateral
stability was well within safety margins.

Blair describes the outcome as a 'deceptively simple and honest
structural solution, enabled by the innovative use of prototyping
technology'. For his part, Clark senses a difference in the way prototypes
are perceived by engineers and architects. For the former, he suggests,
they are mainly for testing performance; for the latter, by contrast, 'every
building is a prototype as it's a one-off … Each sequential building draws
from lessons of the earlier. The prototype is a test.' With *Rock on Top of
Another Rock*, the project team demonstrated the effectiveness of their
digital resources, yet these were employed in the service of producing an
accurately scaled physical prototype to drive the artistic decision-making.

3·33

Marc Fornes & TheVeryMany

Discovering what lies beyond the premise

Marc Fornes & TheVeryMany uses prototypes to test the logistics of production and the logic of assembly. Marc Fornes himself presents each of the practice's beautiful and exacting projects as a failure, saying that they are too long in assembly and require too many small, fine parts. But this is the productive, self-critical form of failure, leading to discovery and faster, tighter processes. Even the prototypes that satisfy their premise uncover some other inefficiency. The studio starts prototyping from the moment it receives a commission. Each prototype sets out to test a premise but throws up the unpredictable – the knowledge that, if gained during the final production run, could have proved disastrous: the colour that cannot be sourced, the curvature that cannot be achieved.

Created as part of Fornes's 2012 residency at the Atelier Calder in Saché, Indre-et-Loire, *Double Agent White* is an architectural installation made from powder-coated aluminium of four different thicknesses. Ranging from 0.024 inches to 0.07 inches, each of these thicknesses behaves differently in terms of possible curvature; the type of aluminium used and the choice of alloy are also important in this regard. The 'Double Agent' of the title refers to the two 'agencies' that worked against each other in the digital generation of the piece. The first was an optimizing agent, which sought to describe the geometry of the work in the minimum number of developable surfaces. The second described the apertures, or cut-out patterns, which also influenced the work's curvature. The overall geometrical schema is nine intersecting spheres of different radii, blended

1 (opposite). *Double Agent White*, Atelier Calder, Saché, Indre-et-Loire, France, 2012: Detail of key drawing created to identify and specify, among other things, components, sequences, aluminium thicknesses and assembled radii of parts of the installation.

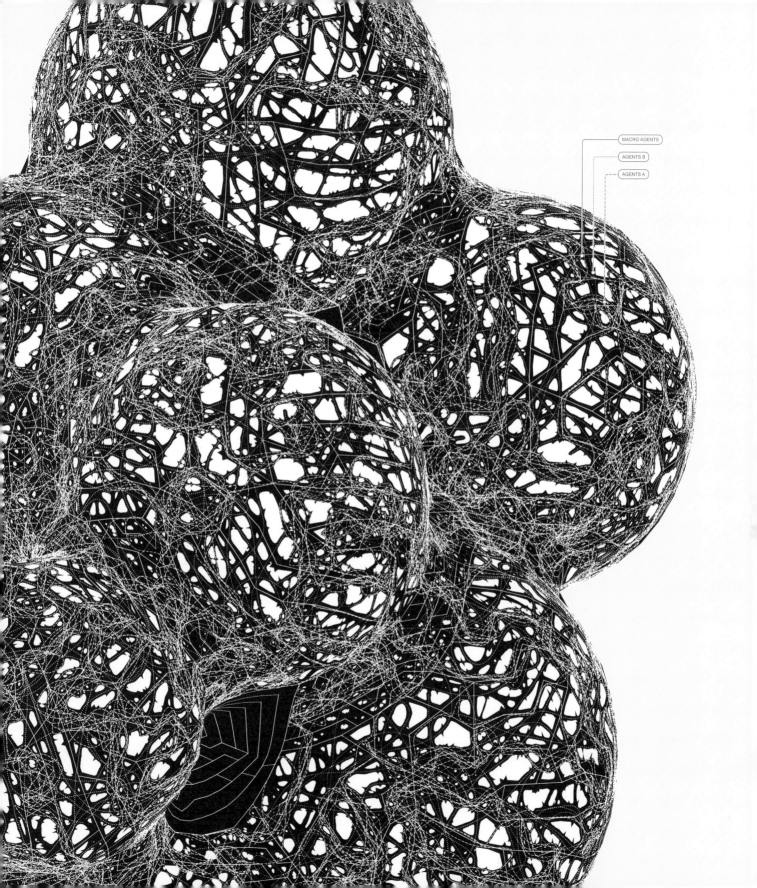

MACRO AGENTS

AGENTS B

AGENTS A

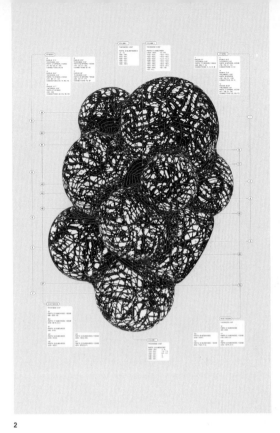

2

3

2. *Double Agent White*: A drawing of
the installation labelled with the names
of individual parts (spheres, columns
and in-betweens) and details of the
installation's construction (radii, thickness
of material, number of sub-parts, etc.).

3. A drawing showing the installation
partially disassembled into 'megaparts'
and 'in-betweens', as well as the parts
packed for shipping.

4 (opposite). Louis Vuitton pop-up shop,
Selfridges, London, 2012: Exploded
isometric drawing.

into a single, doubly curving surface. Made from aluminium less than
a millimetre thick, the individual spheres are quite fragile, even collapsing
under their own weight. But as they come together in the larger assembly,
they become extremely stiff – strong enough, in fact, to bear the weight of
six men. As in the case of many of the practice's installations, prototyping
played a central role in the design and production of the curvature.
Indeed, curvature is key to the practice's work: the tighter it is, the
stronger and stiffer it is.

In contrast to the Atelier Calder installation, Fornes's pop-up shop
for Louis Vuitton, erected in Selfridges in London in 2012, was made
from carbon fibre, a material that had become cost-effective in the way
it could be deployed without moulds. The parameters of the project were
determined by logistics – effectively, a single night in which to assemble
the shop. It had to be delivered to Selfridges at speed, and in the fewest
number of components possible. Moreover, these components had to
have the strength to withstand the rigours of transport, ahead of assembly.

As the practice takes on more projects, and as its portfolio of
completed projects grows, the prototyping is confined to what is new in
each project. At the same time, the projects themselves, while maintaining
the principle of the thin, doubly curved structural skin, become prototypes
for a gradual increase in scale. Performance continues to have its ultimate
test empirically, while the analysis of the complex componentry belies and
generally underestimates the behaviour of the finished products.

Shell E

Shell C

Shell F

Shell B

Shell A

Lamp E

Lamp C

Lamp D

Lamp A

Lamp B

Podium C
Group B / Group B

Podium E
Group A w/Seat / Group A

Podium D
Group B / Group A

Podium A
Group B / Group A w/Seat

Podium B
Group C / Group C

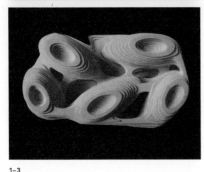

1–3

3·34

← Techniques
2.2 / p. 27 / Mock-ups
2.8 / p. 53 / Virtual Prototyping

Zaha Hadid Architects [Cristiano Ceccato]

A test bed for working out what you are trying to do

1–3. Galaxy Soho, Beijing, China, 2012:
Formal exploration of design concepts
using 3D printing.

4. An artist's impression of the
finished complex.

5. Modelling the surfaces to determine
how many panels would be resolved
to single curvature, and for which panels
double curvature would be required.

According to Cristiano Ceccato, associate director of Zaha Hadid
Architects (ZHA), the practice uses the terms 'test bed' and 'test rig'
to describe a set-up that has many different variants as part of a heuristic
process of updating and testing a design. The prototype is just a particular
version, or moment, in the thinking within this activity – a singular artefact
in a larger process. As you start to learn unexpected things about a
design, says Ceccato, you realize that you are going to have to make many
prototypes. And while models are exploratory, prototypes test the design
as you reach the end of a particular line of thought.

For Ceccato, digital prototyping comes into play at two different
stages in the design process: first, when developing the initial design in
a completely virtual, scaleless, material-less environment; and secondly,
when the design has become more informed and can be given a physical
form. A good example of the challenges involved in making this transition
from the virtual to the real is ZHA's Galaxy Soho (2012), an office, retail and
entertainment complex in the heart of Beijing. Produced using a tightly
controlled digital model, the project's geometry was subject to a multi-
step 'optimization' process intended to simplify it as much as possible
and reduce its cost. At the same time, the architects had to maintain
the underlying design language: there could be no throwing the baby
out with the bath water. Ultimately, the principal constraint was that the
project was going to be clad in sheet metal, using standard-width coils
of aluminium; venturing outside this standard width had the potential

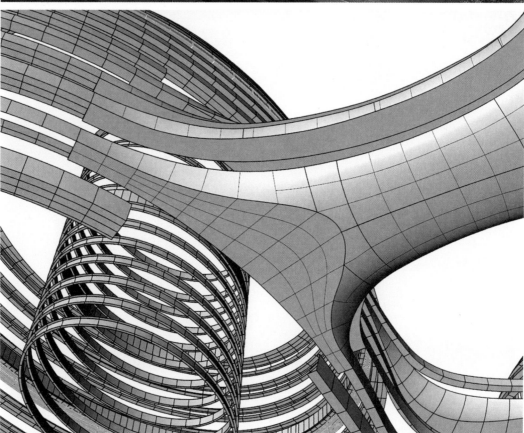

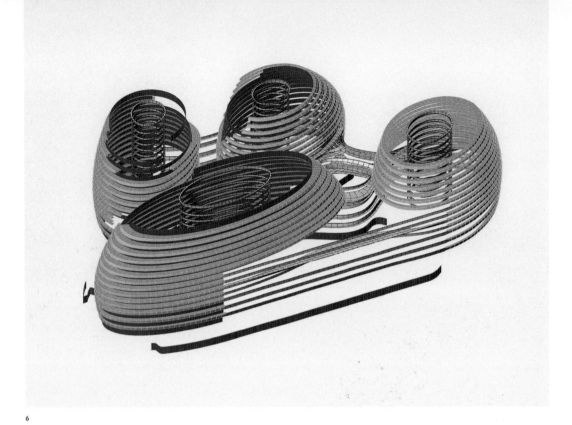

6

to increase wastage, and therefore costs, dramatically. Furthermore, the client had stipulated that, in order to save both time and money, everything had to be manufactured in China. ZHA therefore spent six months travelling the country, visiting the factories of every potential contractor and subcontractor to see what kinds of machinery they had, how they worked, how quickly, and with what level of accuracy. Once the architects had learnt what was possible and had found a solution they could use, the client placed the chosen manufacturing team on the tender list.

Even though ZHA did not have all the answers at the outset, the practice had to have a process that would produce a finished building within budget and on time. Both of these resources were in short supply, and ZHA had to demonstrate continually that it was on track, pushing harder if the client asked it to. Over the course of fifteen months, the design went through four stages of rationalization, from a fluid, 'blobby ball' at the outset to a situation where approximately 98 per cent of the cladding panels were either flat or singly curved surfaces. Doubly curved panels, or those where the curvature went from positive to negative, had to be formed using a mould; everything else could be delivered flat and adjusted on-site. The project's monolithic aesthetic determined a minimum panel size: if the architects had broken the geometry down into ever smaller units, they would have produced a patchwork effect. In addition, there were families of identical components, notably cones. These conic panels could be cut flat without CNC on a simple circle-cutting machine,

6. Galaxy Soho: An early digital prototype.

7–8

9–10

11

7–11. Galaxy Soho: Full-scale, on-site
cladding mock-ups exploring materials,
curvature and finish.

taking advantage of what most Chinese factories could do. In the case of the larger panels, those measuring up to 1,200 × 2,500 millimetres, there could be a deviation of 60–70 millimetres. However, as one reads the curvature of the whole sixteen- and seventeen-storey complex from ground level with the naked eye, this variation cannot be perceived.

There are two major costs associated with prototyping: first, there is the time needed to understand exactly what is being tested and to design the test rig to test it; secondly, there is the manufacture, transport and installation of that rig. In the case of Galaxy Soho, the prototypes for determining the choice of material were organized by the material suppliers themselves, at cost – a dual investment by the client and the fabricator.

Initially, one or two prototype panels were built and kept at ZHA's offices. There were then two rounds of large-scale prototypes. The first was used to determine what the cladding would be made of. Four possibilities presented themselves: sheet metal, formed steel plate, glass-reinforced concrete (GRC) or fibre-reinforced polymer (FRP). For its part, the client insisted on the inclusion of metal, on which it could negotiate the price. A number of boat-builders looked at the steel-plate option, but they would not have been able to deliver on time, and would have had to import machined parts from the Netherlands. FRP was not necessarily technically inferior, but was simply not commercially competitive; in addition, the client had concerns over its fire-rating. In the end, it was an incredibly beautiful mock-up made by the Italian firm Permasteelisa that enabled

12–13

14–15

16

the architects to determine that sheet metal could produce the monolithic appearance demanded by the project's architecture. The prototype was folded in Europe and the United States before being shipped to China.

The second round of prototypes was produced as part of the tendering process. The bids of five potential contractors were composed of three different elements. The first was price, submitted to the client in a sealed envelope. The second was the 'tender return', a set of seven books of shop drawings and details. The third was a physical mock-up of a specified part of the façade. The mock-ups were assessed not only in terms of aesthetics, but also for their underlying structure and how well that would support the building's geometry and result in a smooth, seamless, lump-free form. The client gave each of the contractors an equal stipend for preparing the mock-ups, considered a fair recognition of the cost, but not necessarily covering the full cost of production.

12–16. Galaxy Soho: Full-scale, on-site cladding mock-ups comparing assembly details.

17–19

20 – 21

17–19. Internal views showing
the importance of façade finishing.

20–21. The finished complex,
as seen from different perspectives.

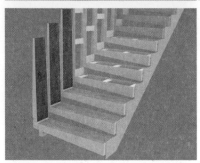

1–2

Facit Homes [Bruce Bell]

Sketching in 3D with real space and real materials

Facit Homes and Wilder Construction work together to design and build bespoke homes. While the branding of the two companies is distinct, their processes are intertwined. Their workshop is littered with hundreds of physical prototypes of the details of components for newly commissioned homes. Old prototypes are bastardized to make new ones, or repurposed as seats and tables. Some of the prototyped details work first time; others reveal the shortcomings of particular strategies or materials in application and lead to a succession of experiments to get everything right. The first physical prototype of a sunshade, for example, highlighted the fact that the steel chosen for its construction was not as rigid as anticipated and needed to be thicker. Some architectural details require a series of prototypes in order to find the optimum design, thereby increasing the amount of investment needed in terms of both time and money. One particular staircase was prototyped first in MDF, secondly in plywood, thirdly in 4-millimetre-thick steel and finally in 6-millimetre-thick steel before being built for installation.

For Bruce Bell, founding partner of Facit Homes, prototyping is sketching, either in 3D or 'in reality'. Coming between the initial concept sketch and the final product, it provides an early opportunity to test and resolve a design. The combination of designer and builder under one roof, with access to its own range of CNC machine tools and spray booth, means that prototyping happens, like production, in-house. Even machining that needs to be outsourced, such as steel cutting or folding,

1–2. Hertfordshire House, UK: Digital mock-ups of the staircase. Facit Homes works with detailed digital mock-ups before proceeding to full-scale physical prototyping.

3–4

5

6

3–5. Hertfordshire House: Installation of the steelwork for the staircase.

6. Detail of the completed balustrade.

is created directly from an in-house digital file, so there is no need for any remodelling or external shop drawing.

Every new detail is prototyped at 1:1. There are no scale models, just virtual walk-throughs created from the 3D computer models for a first-person perspective, and 1:1 prototypes for real-world physicality. Everything the company does involves the computer. The digital workflow and production sequencing is fundamental to its unique business model, and is also prototyped. This system, allowing design changes to ripple down via component design to cutting patterns and machining, is known as the D-process, and it is under continual renewal to further streamline production. Nevertheless, the prototypes themselves are very physical.

In the real world, of course, things can go every so slightly awry. Putting together two 18-millimetre plywood parts cut with a 6-millimetre tool is somehow never as easy in reality as it was on the computer. Variations in texture and surfaces, differences between sheets of the same, engineered timber – none of these things exist in the virtual world. Moreover, a component consisting of fifty different parts can look great when assembled on a computer screen, but when you come to make it, there is an order or sequence in which all these parts need to come together. Usually, this involves banging, twisting or some other form of manual intervention, none of which is easy to simulate accurately in the virtual domain. Experience is the best predictor, but that can sometimes be hard to fall back on when, as Facit Homes does, you are

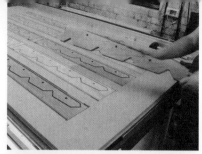

7–9

12–13

10–11

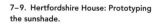
7–9. Hertfordshire House: Prototyping the sunshade.

10–13. A full-scale mock-up of an entire section of the house, complete with windows, sunshade, cladding and lining details, flooring, and internal joinery. Building such a mock-up is a great way to engage the client, while still allowing for change and refinement.

14

continually experimenting and introducing different materials and bespoke architectural details.

Some of the prototypes produced by Facit Homes are for the client, to enable them to choose a colour or material; most, however, are for the company itself, to determine how a design feels, how it has come together – how, if at all, it can be improved. Each of its homes can be seen as a prototype, and each is an improvement on the last. The company's partners have a background in industrial and product design, but have always worked in architecture. One way of looking at their working methods, therefore, is as the application of product design to architecture.

14. The Lodge, Wigginton, Hertfordshire, UK, 2014: Rear view of the completed house.

1–2

3·36

Kreysler & Associates [Bill Kreysler]

A test to measure a design's ability to represent the real world

1. Lawrence Argent, *I See What You Mean*, Colorado Convention Center, Denver, CO, 2005: This 1-metre-tall version of Argent's public art project served as a 'shop drawing' to help the workshop personnel visualize the fabrication process.

2. A Rhino 3D model shows the surfaces to be milled out of the mould, in order to create a 'direct-to-mould' CNC-milled piece mould.

3. CNC-milled tooling produced multiple fibre-reinforced polymer (FRP) 'chips', bonded and assembled into components. Traditional strings and plumb bobs allow accurate alignment.

4. A view inside the partially assembled sculpture reveals the internal bulkhead. Note the 3D 'shop drawing' on the table in the foreground.

Founded in 1981, California-based Kreysler & Associates (K&A) is the world leader in the design and digital fabrication of custom architectural components made from glass-reinforced polymer (GRP). Bill Kreysler transferred his expertise in the building of high-performance racing yachts to the manufacture of an extraordinary range of custom, high-fidelity products that realize their clients' diverse ambitions for finishes, complex geometries and structural gymnastics at minimal weight and environmental impact. The company's work includes the huge, gravity-defying public sculptures of Lawrence Argent and Claes Oldenberg; film sets for such Hollywood blockbusters as the *Star Wars* series and *Minority Report* (2002); the complex interiors of the Louise M. Davies Symphony Hall in San Francisco and Stanford University's Bing Concert Hall; historical façade restorations; and the imaginative architectural geometries of Greg Lynn, Evan Douglis and Snøhetta, for the façades of the San Franscisco Museum of Modern Art (SFMOMA) expansion.

For Kreysler, a prototype is a means of measuring a design's ability to function as intended in the real world. Over the course of more than thirty years, each of the company's projects, to use General Motors' phrase, has been 'for the first time'; to borrow another saying, the company 'practices on its customers', albeit with the provision of a warranty. For most of the unique works that the firm is involved in fabricating, shop drawings are the extent of the prototyping that can be factored into the budget. But because the sketches, photographs and even 3D models that

5–6

7–8

9

5–6. *I See What You Mean:* The sculpture is arranged into shippable components.

7–8. The sculpture's head is checked for assembly in the workshop (fig. 7), and oriented and located on-site.

9. The finished sculpture at the Colorado Convention Center.

it receives from clients often 'raise as many questions as they answer', finished samples are also prepared to ensure that expectations around the all-critical finish and appearance are shared between client and K&A. In effect, each job is prototyped three times. The cost estimate, sometimes a 2,000-line-long spreadsheet, in which the fabrication strategy, materials and assembly process are worked out, is the first prototype; shop drawing ('in excruciating detail') is the second; while the product is the third. The aim is to use the first two forms of prototype to eliminate as much of the risk as possible. Estimating costs is based mainly on experience, but on the fabrication work for the SFMOMA expansion, for example, an intern has been tasked with timing every step of the process. Once the job has been completed, the figures will be compared to those in the estimate, thereby creating a new reference document for costing future work.

Lawrence Argent's *I See What You Mean* (2005), a public artwork created for the Colorado Convention Center in Denver, was digitally prototyped and fabricated. Nevertheless, the work involved great craftsmanship in anticipation of the construction issues involved in erecting a 9-metre-high blue bear. There are many aspects of every job that need to be calculated or simulated, but which are not immediately evident in the 3D computer model. These include, among other things, centre of gravity, moment of inertia, wind loading and strength during lifting.

All materials and material systems have their limitations. When it comes to satisfying the increasing demand in architecture for complex

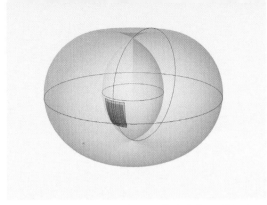

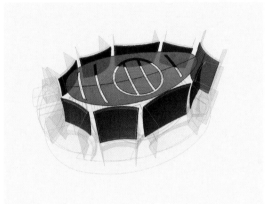

10–11

12–13

shapes, particularly those including double curvature, the composites used by K&A have none of the limitations of sheet metal, for example. They are combustible, however, so the firm has to proceed cautiously with respect to fire codes. In this regard, K&A's use of GRP in its work for the SFMOMA expansion represents a breakthrough for the industry. Agreeing to share the costs with the client, the company undertook to meet the National Fire Protection Association's standard NFPA 285 (Standard Fire Test Method for Evaluation of Fire Propagation Characteristics of Exterior Non-Loadbearing Wall Assemblies Containing Combustible Materials). The combination of K&A's research into the use of fire-resistant resins and the shared speculation on the very expensive testing paid off, opening the door for much more widespread application of GRP in façade design. Prior to this, it would have been impossible to have created the museum façade using composites, even though this is the obvious choice of technology for such a complex surface design.

10–11. Bing Concert Hall, Stanford, CA, 2012: Architect's Rhino 3D model illustrating the rationale for subtracting shapes from the interior of a torus as a means of generating and describing the curvature.

12–13. Wall panel or 'sail' mould used to create panels of a size and weight suitable for shipping to the construction site, but which nevertheless create a flawless surface when assembled on-site.

1–3

3·37

KTA Architects [Kerstin Thompson]

Prototyping tests the qualitative aspects of a design proposal – ahead of tests of performance and constructability

For Kerstin Thompson, director of Melbourne's KTA Architects, the prototype functions more as a means of working things through with the builder than as a device to help the design process along. Moreover, she observes, every building is inherently a prototype of itself, as well as for the next building.

In seeking greater levels of veracity between the proposed architectural approach for a project and the materials and construction methods that will be used for the final building, Thompson argues that the prototype is more effective than the model. While KTA generally makes more models than prototypes for a typical project, it sees the representational qualities of the former as inferior to those of the latter, which, it feels, bring much more precision to the design process.

In KTA's workflow, prototypes are nearly always made at full scale, as this, it has found, has been the only effective way to test certain properties in action. Furthermore, in terms of veracity when probing physical properties, KTA's prototypes are built ideally from the actual materials involved. Models, by contrast, can be made at quite small scales, depending on the what aspect of the design is being explored.

In conversation, Thompson muses on her design process, one in which experimentation and prototyping are the same activity. She goes on to cite a number of examples from her practice where the use of real materials, in their intended context, was absolutely essential to the prototyping of a particular design feature. In the case of the Courtyard

1–3. Courtyard House, Melbourne, Australia: Initial exploration of the lighting effect created by using glass slips in the construction of a brick wall.

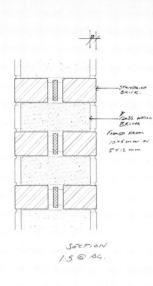

SECTION
1:5 @ A4.

STANDARD BRICK.

GLASS INFILL BRICK FORMED FROM 10×6 mm or 5×12 mm

4

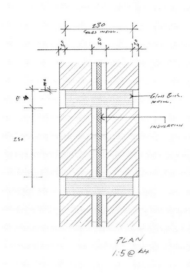

PLAN
1:5 @ A4

Glass Brick Infill.

INSULATION

5

6–7

4–5. Courtyard House: Detailed drawings showing how the glass slips would be used to replace selected perpends in the brick wall.

6–7. The glass slips are placed in the brick wall, first in a trial run (fig. 6) and then in the actual wall.

House in Melbourne, which includes a west-facing brick wall in which selected perpends have been replaced with clear glass slips, this was very much an intuitive move, and not one that drew on her previous experience. This, she says, is an example of where no amount of virtual prototyping would have revealed the effectiveness of such a risky design choice – that is, the fleeting drama of the lowering sun refracting on to the floor through the glass and creating the impression of a pool of water. Not only did the effect go beyond the expectations of the architect, but also it helped to make 'sense of the site', bringing it to life as the sun moved across the sky. Here, the purpose of the prototype was to inform the architect ahead of the builder. Thompson goes on to explain that although she had a hunch about what effect replacing selected vertical mortar joints with glass would have, proof was required all the same.

In the above example, two aspects of the design were being tested through prototyping, initially using dry bricks and glass in the KTA office. First, the effect – would the device actually work? Secondly, the construction – how would it be built? Beyond simple constructability, there were numerous details to consider, such as ensuring an effective seal and the right amount of weathering overhang for the glass, if indeed any overhang was required at all. Thompson observes wryly that while realizing a complex detail might yield surprisingly less challenges than anticipated, other, unexpected problems might emerge out of the blue during the prototyping process. Returning to the example of the brick wall, she

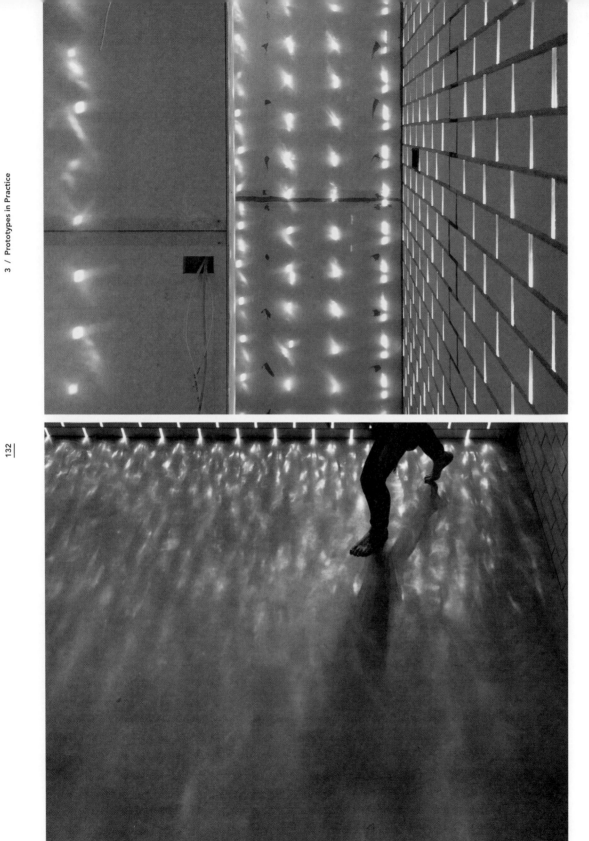

10

11

explains that no one expected that the bricks would chip easily during the extra handling required for the placement of the glass slips.

Thompson states that the practice has been steered towards producing more mock-ups and prototypes than before by an increasingly litigious environment. In terms of client expectations, the hurdles that must be jumped over are higher, with an erosion of credibility with regard to what in previous years amounted to a leap of faith on the client's part: a 'trust me it's going to be magnificent and you've just got to run with it' expectation of the client can no longer be assumed by the architect.

Ultimately, prototyping for Thompson is a means of testing the qualitative or 'atmospheric' aspects of a design proposal ahead of performance and constructability, although she readily concedes that they are equally important but in different respects. Indeed, while the qualitative aspects of a design might be the initial driver for Thompson, she and her colleagues value highly the role of the prototype to explain and prove the feasibility of its construction. Conceding that she undertakes her share of innovation and risk-taking, what she sees as the real tension between architects and builders is the architect's 'wilfulness'. And while she believes that this can be substantially mitigated through prototyping, she is nevertheless driven to get the most from the 'standard way of doing things' – where possible.

8–11. Courtyard House: These views of the wall, both under construction and as built, show the dramatic lighting effects created by the glass slips.

Often, an underlying system of production needs to be designed in order to reach a point where it is possible to produce a first physical, or even virtual, prototype. This system, or network of operations and relationships, may be influenced by many factors – material behaviour, fabrication constraints, formal objectives, choices of technology, the use of automated or manual techniques. The design of the system is, in itself, a process of trial and error in which there are also 'first tries' or 'proto'-types.

In this section of the book we explore a broad range of such system- or workflow-prototyping paradigms. The first example transfers a digital parametric model of a surface effect directly to the building site in order to work out how to translate, notate and, at the same time, control the built version through an interface with highly traditional craft-based construction. The second takes material behaviour as its point of departure and explores how best to transpose physical discovery into the digital realm in order to create something new.

Cooperation between software engineers and designers is an interesting way to cultivate digital systems for better modelling in construction. The use of a broad mix of design, computing, construction and business expertise in a highly controlled framework to produce extraordinary architecture from constrained briefs is something at which SHoP Architects has excelled through their rigorous prototyping of systems. Finally, the sacrificial 'artist's prototype' and the careful choice of technology to achieve the desired outcome are also important contributors to well-designed design-to-production workflows.

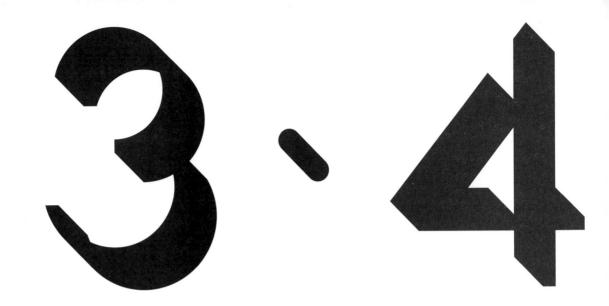

3·4

Prototyping Workflow Processes

1–2

← Techniques
2.1 / p. 23 / Traditional Techniques
2.2 / p. 27 / Mock-ups
2.8 / p. 53 / Virtual Prototyping

Archi-Union

Prototyping construction processes: materiality and tradition

For Philip F. Yuan, founding principal of Shanghai-based architectural practice Archi-Union, the key to prototyping in architecture is to take into account both materiality and tradition. Archi-Union's own studio, known as the 'J-Office' (2010), exemplifies this approach. The three former textile warehouses that make up the studio are enclosed on three sides by a new wall. Redolent of the textiles once stored at the site, the wall takes as its motif billowing silk. This subtle effect has been achieved using the simplest and most traditional of materials and techniques.

Although an industrial robot can now be found among the designers at Archi-Union, the practice has not restricted itself to the pick-and-place bricklaying operations pioneered by Gramazio Kohler Architects. This is evidenced by the new wall, which is intended to explore the opportunities and constraints that arise when working with a human workforce with traditional bricklaying skills. The project was centred around the development of a semi-automated templating and notational system for the translation of such variable phenomena as undulating silk into a simple serial task to be executed within a traditional craft context.

The wall itself consists of low-cost hollow breeze blocks, which were laid at varying angles – as determined by an algorithmic model – to create a rippling effect. The prototyping took place as part of the actual construction process, with feedback from such construction issues as the displacement of the breeze blocks re-informing the model. The number of different angles at which the blocks were laid was limited to ten, while

1–4. J-Office, Shanghai, China, 2010: Simple plywood templates were used to control the angle of placement of the individual breeze blocks, as determined by the digital model. The resulting effect is that of billowing silk.

5–10

-10   -5   0   5   10

-90   0   +90

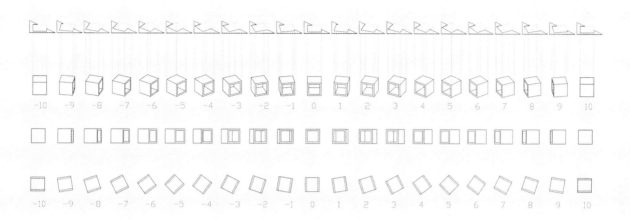

-10 -9 -8 -7 -6 -5 -4 -3 -2 -1 0 1 2 3 4 5 6 7 8 9 10

-10 -9 -8 -7 -6 -5 -4 -3 -2 -1 0 1 2 3 4 5 6 7 8 9 10

11

5–10. J-Office: Views of the wall at various stages of construction.

11. Diagram showing the configuration of a single row of breeze blocks and the templates used to position them. A finite number of angles produced highly variable effects across the whole wall.

the model was adjusted to produce a less extreme but nevertheless silk-like ripple. A similar design and construction process was used by Archi-Union for the Lanxi Curtilage at the International Intangible Cultural Heritage Park in Chengdu, China, where varied brick spacing and a combination of materials imbue the wind-permeable wall with rich textile qualities.

Composed of a modular bamboo mesh, the walls – or 'energy skin' – of the Para Eco-House also feature a wind-permeable design. The house was built in 2012 by a team of students from Tongji University for the second Solar Decathlon Europe, an international competition designed to promote the development of energy-efficient buildings, and features an integrated system of passive and active technologies, including photovoltaic panels, a green roof and a water-treatment system. In this case, the whole house acted as a prototype, not only showcasing the latest developments in green technology but also exploring, at full scale, the performance of the house and the way in which people interacted with it.

While prototyping in architecture is essentially the same as that in industry and manufacturing, the architectural profession, as Yuan notes, has been relatively slow in its deployment of the technology. Yet its potential benefits are numerous. The use of automated fabrication, for example, could drastically reduce the number of people needed on a building site. Architecture students are, however, beginning to think of new ways of working, including much greater integration between off-site fabrication and on-site assembly.

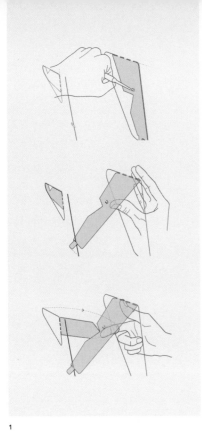

1

3·42

← Techniques
2.4 / p. 37 / CNC Revolution
2.8 / p. 53 / Virtual Prototyping

Marble Fairbanks [Scott Marble]

Prototyping a process leading to workflow

1. Flatform, Museum of Modern Art, New York, NY, 2008: An illustration showing the procedure for folding and locking the sheet material into place.

2–8. A series of laser-cut metal prototypes intended to explore and develop possible 'slot and tab' mechanisms.

Scott Marble asks the question, how can you prototype a process? He supplies his own, partial answer: workflow. The question of how to prototype design and production processes, particularly those of the digital variety, has been of particular interest to Marble for a number of years. The design studios he has run with students at Columbia University in New York have taken up this question, leading to the creation of a library of prototypes – little pieces of carefully crafted digital design that anyone can now use and build on.

Marble names Renzo Piano's practice, which has been working on a new campus at Columbia and a new home for the Whitney Museum of American Art, as an example of a long-established practice to which prototypes and mock-ups are central. Each time the practice is engaged by a client, it is assumed that it is going to break boundaries, and that this will happen through an intense process of physical prototyping and testing. There are only a few architects who can do this, and the practice's work represents a powerful argument against those who see architecture as product. In general, it is quite hard for an architect to take clients on this journey, to convince them that, in effect, they should act as guinea-pigs in the design process; that rather than asking to see what the designer has produced before, they should fund a process of experimentation, prototyping and, most expensive of all, construction of full-scale mock-ups.

The work of New York-based practice Marble Fairbanks takes process as a philosophical and practical point of departure. It has worked its digital

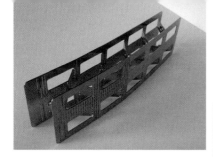

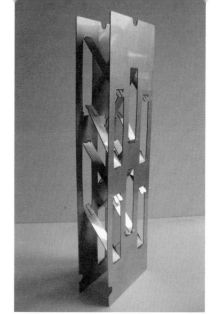

2–4

5–6

7–8

9–10

11

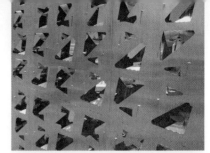

12–13

142

9–13. Flatform: Installation views at the
Museum of Modern Art, New York, 2008.

14–15. Exploratory digital prototypes
of folded sheet-metal arrays.

workflow hard over the years, but also cleaves to the belief that until
you create a physical prototype, it is not possible fully to understand what
you have. A prototype tests the reality of something. It is also a matter
of degree of precision.

In the case of an industrial object, there are usually dozens of
prototypes, culminating in a more or less one-to-one correspondence
between intent and result. With buildings, however, the gap tends to
be greater, with more unknowns until the building has actually been built.
There is a fundamental difference, in other words, in the level of precision.
Marble Fairbanks' Flatform project for the Museum of Modern Art in New
York – an exploration of design and assembly – provided the practice with
an opportunity to work at the level of precision associated with industrial
production. The focus was again on process, but one led by material.

With both the Flatform project and the Toni Stabile Student Centre
at Columbia, the aesthetics were considered the result of the production:
the CNC machining and production constraints contributed to the design
concept. Marble says that the practice will often decide to work in a
material, stainless steel for example, or deploy a technique, ahead even
of the design. They start prototyping straight away, getting little samples
back from the fabricator and learning all the properties of a material, and
that information becomes conceptually fundamental to the design and the
design process. There is merit in staying uncomplicated, in taking simple
ideas and engaging in those ideas very, very deeply.

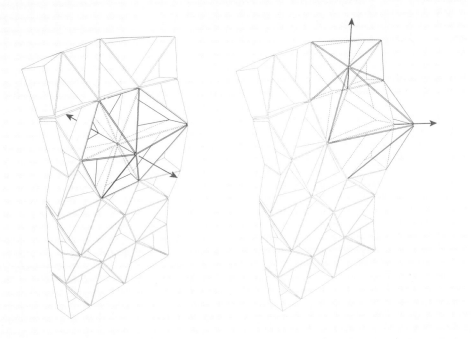

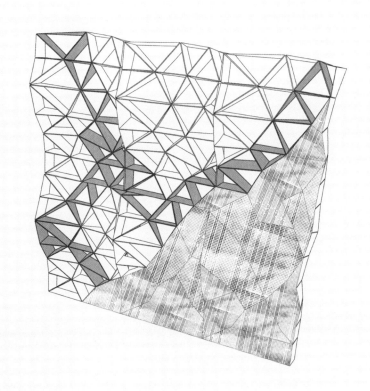

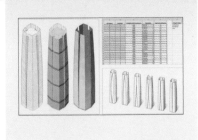

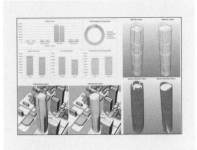

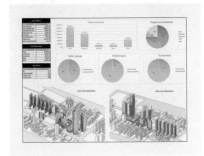

1–3

1–3. Prototyping automated data generation for rapid comparative feedback with regard to different tower designs.

3·43

← Techniques
2.3 / p. 31 / Prototyping Performance
2.8 / p. 53 / Virtual Prototyping

CASE Inc.

Prototyping architectural software tools

For Steve Sanderson, partner at CASE, the distance between a prototype and a functional product is becoming increasingly small. As a building information modelling (BIM) consultancy, CASE develops software tools for the construction industry, as well as some utilities that it gives away online. The time it takes for an initial concept for a piece of software to move from a wireframe sketch to a functional prototype can be incredibly short. In other words, the prototype is a usable version of the software while the final version is still being developed. This use of 'agile' software development, a highly adaptive and flexible form of development, contrasts with the traditional 'waterfall' process, in which detailed specifications serve as the foundation for a rigid, sequential development process, ending with the launch of a complete and 'bombproof' solution.

CASE's use of 'agile' protocols is indicative of a shift in the approach to modelling in the architecture, engineering and construction (AEC) sector. The idea that you can take a single model through from a powerful napkin sketch to construction documents and fabrication is one that many of today's architectural-practice principals have grown up with and, indeed, cling to. It is also one that has been used as a marketing platform by BIM software vendors. But architectural models need not be seen as perfect, refined products. Models that serve an intended purpose and have a finite lifespan – allowing you, if you so wish, to start again at the end of a design phase – can lead to a more 'agile' approach in AEC too. Sanderson, for one, is very much in favour of the model fit for purpose.

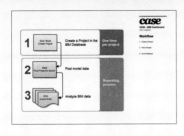

4–7

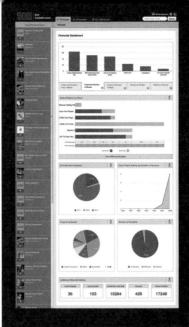

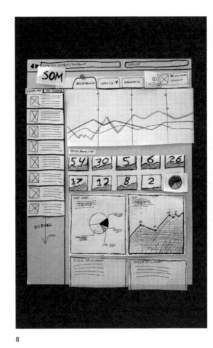

8

9

4–7. Linking building
information modelling (BIM)
data to prototyping projects.

8. SOM: 'Paper wireframe',
or mock-up, of the dashboard.

9. A screenshot of the completed
program, showing firm-wide data.

CASE is more or less equally divided between designers with an interest in software and software engineers with or without a background in the construction sector. For their part, the designers have come from a practice background in which it was customary to look to the aerospace or shipbuilding industries, for example, for the direction in which AEC might move next. At CASE, however, they are focused on using the agility of the booming start-up culture in New York as the model for innovation.

The divide between software engineers and designers highlights the differences between a software design process and a building design process. Those with a formal software engineering background know how to work together with other developers in order to provide all the expertise they need for a larger software project. The architect/engineers have more of a tradition of working alone, using their time to discover the design parameters of a problem.

A key to the fast transition from an initial idea to a usable prototype is setting out the parameters within which it is expected to work. As with an industrial prototype, the end goal should be very clear – for example, to make a process faster. On the other hand, architects use the tools available to them in a way that allows them to define the end goal as they go along. This is a more ambiguous and exploratory process, so access to a prototype is very important in enabling the users of a software tool to articulate exactly what it is that they want to get out of it. As soon as they start using the prototype, the conversation becomes more productive.

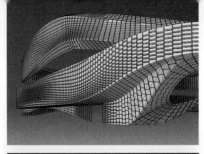
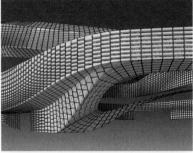
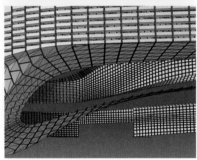

1–3

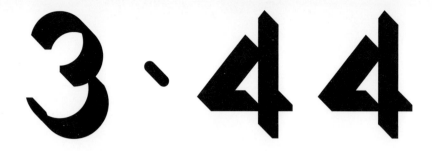

← Techniques
2.3 / p. 31 / Prototyping Performance
2.4 / p. 37 / CNC Revolution
2.8 / p. 53 / Virtual Prototyping

SHoP [Chris Sharples]

Physical and virtual prototyping is simply a given throughout the entire project-development cycle

SHoP is the go-to practice when looking for an alternative to traditional practice and a range of design and fabrication skills that take full advantage of each new digital opportunity as it emerges. Since 1996 the New York-based practice has been a global leader in innovation and the uptake of new technology to the extent that it now runs as two parallel operations: SHoP Architects and SHoP Construction. According to its website, it 'thrives on constraints', approaching every new project with 'open minds' and 'an expert team'. Together, the two divisions are upfront about pushing such real-world constraints as budgets and schedules – the consideration of which is at the heart of any creative practice. In so doing, SHoP offers its clients a fresh and coherent approach to building procurement. Prototyping is key to everything it does and, unsurprisingly, has become a hallmark of its originality and effectiveness.

Renowned for its 1:1 design studies produced en route to the final outcome, SHoP sees prototyping as the pathway to the mock-up, a journey that ends in a successful, fully evaluated project prior to its construction. Prototyping for the practice might involve the creation of literally hundreds of iterations along the way, but their intention is always to produce just the one mock-up at the end, as a conclusion to the design process – a verification of all that has gone before in the quest to marry aesthetic, constructional, economic and logistical objectives. This, it finds, allows both the creative team and the client to be completely confident that the resulting proposal is the optimal one from all points of view.

1–3. Barclays Center, Brooklyn, NY, 2012: Virtual prototyping of the overall building form and tessellated exterior surface. The design of the overall form went through more than a hundred iterations during the development cycle.

4–7. 3D-printed prototypes of a section of the cantilevered canopy, showing the tessellated exterior surface.

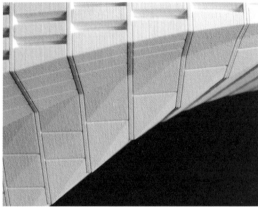

4–5

6–7

The distinction between models, prototypes and mock-ups is therefore very clear to the practice; whatever aspect of the design the prototype is focusing on, it need not shoulder the burden of all of the prospective building's performance challenges. Whereas a mock-up deals with real conditions – the effects of such applied forces as gravity, the way light strikes the surfaces, how the design comes together as a constructed artefact – prototypes can test quite a narrow set of attributes without presuming to test the whole.

Virtual prototyping for SHoP is a crucial part of its workflow. However, it treats it as being quite distinct from physical prototyping, literally adding one or more dimensions into the mix, such as time (4D prototyping) or time and cost (5D prototyping). Whereas physical prototyping focuses predominantly on physical testing, virtual prototyping is able to look at such intangibles as workflow, especially construction and associated costs. This ability to prototype a project in such depth is one of the qualities that gives SHoP its distinguishing edge. And although the degree of precision it is able to provide early on in the design process is not necessarily definitive, it gives the client an earlier and clearer sense of where the project is heading.

Since prototyping is integral to the services provided by SHoP, there is no question of it being an additional cost to be borne by either the client or the practice. While the practice is not explicit about its approach and methodology in terms of client engagement, having positioned itself

8

8. Barclays Center: The 25-metre cantilevered canopy, seen here under construction, was designed to deflect by 0.5 metres. Once completed, the canopy was scanned so as to fine-tune the bracket design and placement. Indeed, the entire building process was virtually prototyped.

9–10. Views of the completed building. The exterior surface is clad in 12,000 uniquely sized panels.

as being especially motivated by highly constrained projects and contexts, the prominent role of prototyping throughout its engagement in any project is simply a given: it's what SHoP does.

This is not, however, as straightforward as it might sound. The practice is able to work in this way now because of a financially painful decision it took when it first set out: to develop its prototype-based workflow within a conventional fee structure. It was only by having the confidence to invest in a radically different design (and ultimately construction) workflow that its credibility as alternative practitioners could be established. Working directly with fabricators and developing the trust of others to push efficiency and economic gains through the introduction of 'file to factory' protocols are also aspects of SHoP's working methods that had to evolve through practice, not theory.

Perhaps it is the separation of the company into SHoP Architects and SHoP Construction that has promoted a distinction between physical and virtual prototyping across the two divisions. Research and development has been and remains pivotal to SHoP's evolution, and it is clear from the resulting projects why its highly sophisticated approach to prototyping strategies brings rewards to all those involved.

9–10

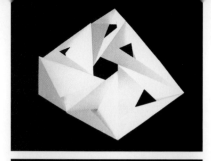
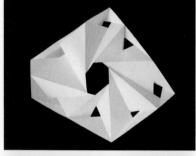
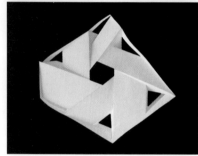

1–3

3 · 4 5

← Techniques
2.1 / p. 23 / Traditional Techniques
2.4 / p. 37 / CNC Revolution
2.8 / p. 53 / Virtual Prototyping

Aranda\Lasch [Ben Aranda]

Prototyping modular systems

1–3. Palais des Art, Libreville, Gabon, 2013–: Folded-paper models exploring potential reciprocal structural solutions for the roof of the outdoor theatre.

4 (opposite). A cardboard model of the Palais des Art site, showing the theatre (left) and the Palais de Banquet.

A prototype is a way to be predictive about how things act. You may prototype not just how something works, but also a range of effects. For Aranda\Lasch, a design practice with offices in New York and Tuscon, Arizona, prototyping has been central to its exploration of systems that are modular, scalable and controlled through computation. There is a dialogue in its work between architectural design and designing and producing at the scale of furniture and installation. Furniture design, for the practice, is a way to prototype architectural ideas.

The artist's (or architect's) prototype (AP) has its idiosyncrasies. It is not, for example, something its creator would want to be put on sale. Rather, it is used to generate interest, and as the basis for the finished article. While produced for testing purposes, the AP also has an intrinsic value, and can sometimes find its way into an exhibition, such as Aranda\Lasch's 'Rose Chair' exhibited at New York's Museum of Arts and Design.

Compared to furniture, architecture represents a huge investment for the person or institution commissioning it. As practice co-founder Ben Aranda reflects, a prototype does not really give you the opportunity to understand a building fully. The project to design the Palais des Art in Libreville, Gabon, was awarded to Aranda\Lasch in an international competition. A collaborative project with structural engineers AKT II, it includes the creation of an outdoor theatre. The theatre's highly innovative design consists of a canopy made from long panels of the local hardwood that act as both primary and secondary structure.

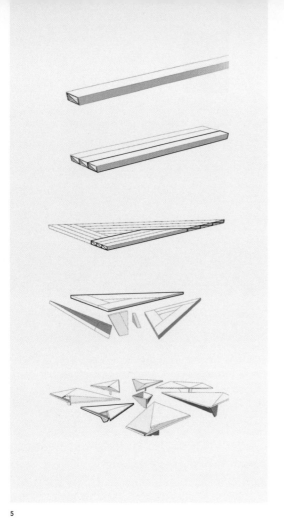

5

6

5–6. Palais des Art: Diagrams of the
reciprocal roof structure for the outdoor
theatre, showing the timber patterning
and assembly.

7–9. Computer renderings of the
completed theatre.

7–9

10–12

13–14

10–12. Quasitable, New York, NY, 2007–:
Assembling two types of rhomboid walnut
block with reference to the aperiodic formation
of quasicrystals. The table came together
from a series of complex subassemblies.

13–14. The table is composed of 3,000
individual walnut blocks, hand-assembled
with extreme precision.

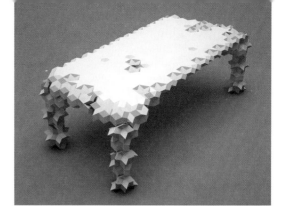

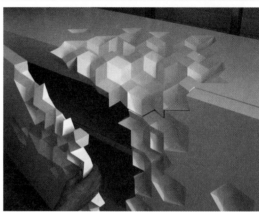

15–16

17–18

15. Quasitable: Exploded view showing the process of construction and assembly.

16. A 3D print of the geometric thinking behind the design process.

17. A computer rendering of the final design.

18. Quasicabinet, New York, NY, 2007–: The principles behind the design of the Quasitable were used to create this cabinet.

A very different commitment to investigating modular systems is the Quasitable (2007–), a large dining table made from hundreds of individual blocks of walnut. Although Aranda\Lasch mocks up every piece of furniture at 1:1, it was decided that, given the scale and ambition of the project, the built prototype would be a single leg. The whole table was so difficult to make that the architects' initial reaction was that it would be the last time they would try anything similar. The difficulties led to the re-engineering of the entire process of assembly for subsequent output. Aranda emphasizes the importance of failure in relation to prototyping. The table was not a failure per se – it enabled the practice to show that it was possible to build an object using a process based on the irregular formation of quasicrystals, and was sold to a happy collector – but it was simply too complicated for a few people working by hand to produce within a reasonable amount of time. 'We love that table,' observes Aranda, 'but it nearly killed us.'

For the second version of the table, the practice used milled-out 3D moulds as a template in which to place the timber units in order to orient them. They created aggregations of cells around foam shells that eliminated the issue of 'suicidally' inadequate tolerances in the first system. Happily, the practice's fascination with applying procedural thinking to small modular parts survived the manual prototyping ordeal that was the first Quasitable.

1–2

3·46

SIAL [Nicholas Williams]

Refinement beyond the single project

1–4. FabPod, Design Hub, RMIT University, Melbourne, Australia, 2013: The FabPod prototype was created in response to the challenge of designing a meeting room for open-plan work environments.

In architecture, prototyping can be extended beyond the single project to include the examination of processes, details or ideas in the context of several projects. Prototyping really starts when the design is narrowed down and reaches a stage of refinement. Prototypes are distinguished by their investigation of built performance; models, on the other hand, represent ideas that might sit slightly outside the design-development process.

Digital prototyping involves prototyping the digital workflow, the structure for a whole series of investigative models and, in some cases, performance (although real testing often leads back to the physical prototype). Even digital information systems need to be prototyped. In architecture, the constraints, rules and degrees of freedom needed in the digital parametric model of a design are influenced by physical production processes. Previously, constructing variable and unique architectural geometries required the building of unique jigs, one after the other. Today, however, there is an assumption that a CNC machine will have a variable jig 'built in', with the geometries and degrees of freedom of that jig first defined and programmed in the parametric model.

The biggest change in prototyping in recent years has been the increased accessibility of computer-aided manufacturing (CAM). The technical barriers to using CNC milling machines and three-axis routers have fallen away, and the process is now much closer to 'plug-and-play'. However, while designers have become more like makers, there is some

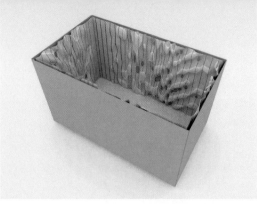
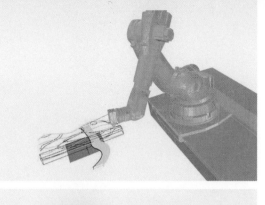

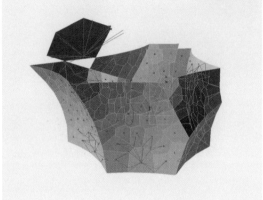

5–6

7–8

5–6. The Music Room: Conceptual-design images relating component fabrication to patterning strategies at a larger scale.

7. Prototyping the use of novel robotic bandsaw cutting to produce the surface patterning (see also figs 9–10).

8. FabPod: first virtual prototype testing custom cell distribution on intersecting spherical surfaces.

loss of appreciation of the fact that the machines and processes have developed in an industrial context, and of the underlying factors that affect speed, precision and degrees of freedom. Not everyone understands how to take advantage of, say, the increased geometrical capacities of a five-axis router over a three-axis machine. The tension between exploration and refinement should be productive, and a broad community has a role to play. For example, a lot of detailed CNC knowledge is now coming from amateur experts in the maker community, who are 3D printing in their living rooms on a daily and experimental basis.

In architectural projects, work is carried out at different scales, one of which is the scale of the whole system, to describe and deliver a design from concept to components and assembly. This was exemplified by the design, production and assembly of custom cells for the FabPod meeting room. At a larger scale, prototyping is much more about the experience of the space and broader performance and perceptual issues. In the case of both the FabPod and the Music Room, a music practice room for a school, such issues included acoustics, which were simulated digitally to drive the form and materiality of the design. Both projects, on which Nicholas Williams has worked closely with architect John Cherrey, are prototypes in their own right. Both have been extensively physically prototyped, not only for acoustic properties but also to explore finish; with the Music Room, this involved a series of novel tests using a robot and a bandsaw blade to achieve different cross-grain effects with different timbers.

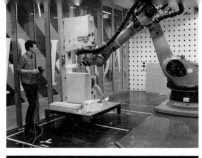

9-10

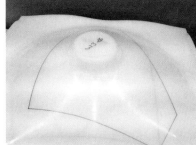

11-14

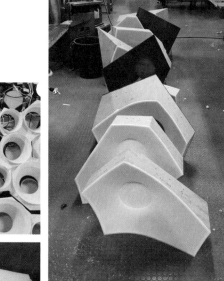

15-16

9-10. The Music Room: Prototyping
the use of novel robotic bandsaw cutting
to produce the surface patterning.

11-16. FabPod: Early prototype cells
are tested for fabrication tolerances
and acoustic properties.

When prototyping is taken to be a deliberate and discrete activity within the design process, it is reasonable to assume that it occurs at some point between the creation of the design model and the building of the project. These are situations where the function of the model is purely representational, whereas the prototype is the first thing that is built specifically to inform the design process as it goes along.

In all the examples in this section, the prototype is treated as the site of enquiry. In some cases, as with the examples drawn from Arup and MOS Architects, the prototype can be a melding of both virtual and physical testing. In others, such as the work of Studio Gang, the 'later stage' prototype is used more empirically than a prototype engaged earlier in the design process would be.

Despite the prototype being the first thing to be built in many of the examples discussed here, the level of its 'finished-ness' depends very much on where in the design process it appears, to the extent that, in some cases, it can barely be distinguished from a 1:1 mock-up. As observed in the Hopkins Architects entry, a prototype can be defined in at least three different ways: first, as something initiated within the studio to make an early link between design and manufacturing; secondly, as a pre-tender exposé of construction issues; and thirdly, as something produced post-contract to ease the 'constructability' conversation between architect and builder.

In terms of the relationship between the prototype and the building it informs – regardless of where it appears in the design cycle or the degree of its finished-ness – in the examples in this section, the prototype is the first thing you build.

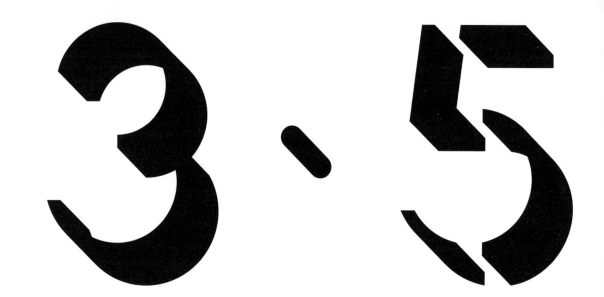

3 . 5

The First Thing You Build

← Techniques
2.2 / p. 27 / Mock-ups
2.3 / p. 31 / Prototyping Performance

Arup [Hugo Mulder]

The first thing that you build

For Arup engineer Hugo Mulder, a prototype is the first thing you build that is not the actual thing that you are going to build. It is a model constructed to test something in the real world – the first realization of an otherwise digital or virtual object. Mulder believes that you cannot test physical properties in a digital environment; the reality, however, is that prototyping will increasingly involve the digital and the physical working together.

Mulder cites an example of a project where the construction of a prototype was essential: the High Roller observation wheel in Las Vegas – currently the world's tallest – for which Arup was engaged to provide a variety of design and engineering services. Because the wheel was going to be used in high temperatures, the glass of the cabins had to be insulated in order to keep the interiors cool. The only way to test the specialist glass required for the cabins was to have a prototype made. Despite the costs involved, the client was willing to pay for a prototype because the proper functioning of the cabins was critical to the success of the overall design. A prototype was duly made, tested, and visually inspected by the client.

Firms that specialize in the building of moving structures are well accustomed to prototyping. There are many aspects of such structures that, before construction can begin, must be tested in a real-world environment, such as wear and tear on moving parts. In the case of the London Eye, the relatively fast rotation of the wheel meant that it was

1 (opposite). High Roller observation wheel, Las Vegas, NV, 2014: Measuring 167.6 metres in height, the High Roller is the world's tallest observation wheel.

2–3

4–5

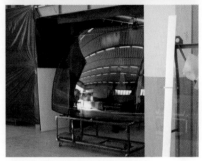

6–7

2–7. High Roller: The client and
representatives from Arup inspect
prototypes of the cabin glass in Padua,
Italy, in 2011. The prototypes were
being checked for colour, distortion
and reflection.

8–9. The completed wheel, as seen
at platform level and from the ground.

necessary to test the ease or otherwise of getting into and out of the
cabins as they passed the boarding ramp. Local residents were asked
if they wished to participate in the testing process.

In general, building contractors have a tradition of doing things
a certain way, instinctively resisting anything that deviates from the
norm, including the use of the latest prototyping technology. However,
this reluctance to try new things is often put to one side in the case of
specialist or very challenging projects, where there is more of an incentive
to build a prototype. Contractors for the High Roller had to test, among
other things, the integrity of the water seals and the operation of the
cabins' doors; in the case of the latter, this meant putting them through
rigorous 'operational cycles', in which the doors were made to open and
close approximately 10,000 times. It was also necessary to test the cabins
in a climate chamber, where they were blasted with sand to simulate the
desert conditions of the Las Vegas area. Some major contractors have their
own facilities for testing; others have to use external laboratories.

Mulder argues that prototyping makes the design process much
easier, which, in turn, means that you can start building a lot sooner than
would otherwise be the case. For one thing, you do not need to have
finished a design before building a prototype, since the prototype allows
you to revisit the design and adjust it as you go along. Furthermore, trying
something a couple of times gives you greater insight into the design
process itself.

1–3

Hopkins Architects [Michael Taylor]

A dry run before the real thing

1–3. Velodrome, Olympic Park, London, 2011: Prototyping the connection brackets for the net of steel cable (see below).

4 (opposite). The doubly curved roof of the Velodrome is formed by a net of steel cable. The net is composed of paired 36-millimetre-diameter galvanized-steel cables, clamped together at 3.6-metre centres. Each clamp was positioned at ground level using marks made when the cables were pre-stressed and cut to size in the factory. Connection brackets were then secured to each clamp before the net was lifted into position and stretched to connect to a ring beam.

A prototype enables the designer to sample part of their design ahead of time. It can lead to refinement or warn of a potential failure. As a dry run, the prototype can be broken down into three categories. The first is the prototype initiated in the design studio to help understand the design and manufacturing processes better. The second is the pre-tender prototype, created to inform the 'what' and 'how' of construction; the client might pay for these directly. The third category is the prototype initiated with or by the contractor to show how something might be manufactured, installed or integrated into the construction process. Timing is everything: the earlier you make a prototype, the more informative and influential it will be on the final outcome; the later you leave it, by contrast, the better the information you will have to incorporate in the test.

One prototype will not serve every purpose. In the case of Hopkins Architects' Frick Chemistry Laboratory at Princeton University (2010), the contractor built a detailed mock-up of a window bay, complete with blinds, after the façade contract had been awarded, when the frame of the building was up but with change still possible. The prototype proved very useful, allowing architect and client to evaluate the detail, and the contractor to communicate with the subcontractor. But in order to do a proper wind-pressure test on the façade, a completely different panel had to be manufactured and taken to Permasteelisa in Italy to be tested in front of a large turbine.

5–6

7–8

9–10

5–8. Velodrome: Each connection bracket has four receiver brackets that support the roof panels via steel shoes built into the corners of each panel. Every roof panel is secured with one fixed, one slotted and two over-sized receiver brackets, allowing movement but keeping panels orthogonal to the cable net.

9–10. Frick Chemistry Laboratory, Princeton University, NJ, 2010: Performance-testing mock-ups.

There are limitations to the feedback a designer can get from a prototype. In fact, a prototype will not solve all their problems, but it can begin to highlight where the problems might be. Integral to any prototype is a sense of function: it needs to work at some level, to be more than a visual mock-up. One of the principal benefits of the prototype is that it enables the designer to find out not only if their design works but also how it looks – although no one else on the project team will care about the aesthetics. In some cases, it may even allow the designer to change its appearance, sometimes by subterfuge.

No one really wants to pay for prototypes, which are often seen as an expense rather than a tool to increase efficiency and reduce risk. This can make them difficult to incorporate into the design and construction process. When margins are tight and the contractor is short of time, a typical scenario might be to agree to prototype the corner of a building, but with the intention of leaving it there and including it in the final works. This can create tension around change and refinement.

In architectural practice, designers now have access to many different ways of testing elements quickly, such as 3D CAD and digital fabrication, but labour costs are higher, buildings are built more quickly and builders are more risk-averse. A familiar attitude is: 'We are all for innovation, but we just don't want to be the first to try it.'

11–12

13–14

11–14. Velodrome: The prefabricated timber gutter cassette forms the junction between the roof and the façade. There are seventeen cassette sizes, with a range of standardized and bespoke prefabricated units and perimeter make-up pieces fabricated on-site.

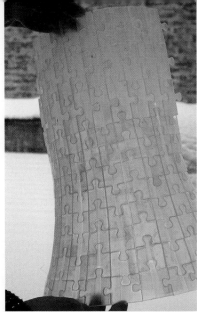

1–2

Studio Gang [Jeanne Gang]

Taking specific liberties through prototyping

For Jeanne Gang, founder of architects Studio Gang, the prototype is something of a movable feast. If it is intended to test structure, for instance, it could come some way down the design process, close to the eventual outcome. Equally, however, she believes that a prototype can be useful far earlier in the process, and somewhat more experimental in nature. Early prototypes will typically look less finished compared with those that are used to inform the completed building. Later-stage prototypes designed to test aspects of structural and thermal performance have an empirical aspect to them, whereas the earlier, experimental kind are often testing more abstract phenomena.

Models, in contrast to prototypes, go further as design tools for Studio Gang, which uses them to elicit intent and to evoke a feeling about a project. Although some of the models it makes along the way are used to test such practical aspects of a design as materials, they tend to be more concerned with the artistic side of things. When producing models, the practice takes much bigger liberties with design than when creating prototypes, which they tend to keep quite specific and focused in order to ensure that they remain useful at a practical level. Scaling up a model generates a different set of design considerations from those associated with the full-size prototype, which is moving towards something real: the completed building.

When it comes to the practice taking liberties, the Marble Curtain (2003) – a 5.5-metre-tall stone curtain intended to test the strength of

1–2. Marble Curtain, National Building Museum, Washington DC, 2003: Prototypes showing the 'jigsaw' design of the curtain using smaller pieces of marble than originally proposed.

3 (opposite). Installation view of the completed curtain at the National Building Museum, Washington DC.

4–5

6

7

4–7. Writers Theater, Glencoe, IL, 2013–: Full-scale mock-ups of the structural system for the façade.

stone in tension – is a prime example. Gang recalls a drawn-out process of prototyping with a wide variety of materials, physically testing them until they broke. Different geometries were tested precisely for each of the interlocking pieces of the curtain. This involved a certain amount of computer scripting to ensure particular constraints were factored in, such as checking that the bearing shoulders of the joints were sufficiently robust, especially given that all the pieces were unique. Material performance parameters were also built into the computer-script testing, for both the physical performance and a conforming geometry – that is, a geometrical configuration that works. Even the vertical structural joints required testing, in order to determine which type of silicone adhesive to use.

In such novel projects as Marble Curtain, it is necessary to test every aspect of the design. Surprises can happen along the way, bringing about quite significant shifts in direction. In the case of Marble Curtain, it was assumed that 30- to 60-centimetre stone tiles would be available from which to craft the individual pieces; however, it later transpired that the larger sizes were in fact not available. Only through the script were radical changes possible, prompting the thought that scripting in this context could be considered as prototyping.

Gang turns to the subject of the changing attitudes of clients towards the use of prototypes. In the context of her own practice, she points to the Writers Theater (2013–) in Glencoe, Illinois, as an example of a project where circumstances dictated a request for the client to meet additional

8–9

10–11

12

design-investigation costs. As the project got underway, it became clear that timber would be the best material for its construction. But it was further along in the process before a particular type of timber could be identified and assessed. Keen to use very thin timber members to support the walkway, the client engaged a specialist engineer. Their employment could not have been predicted at the outset – adventurous prototyping mid-design had led to an unexpected technical challenge and, as a consequence, supplementary testing of the emerging joint design. One senses with a practice like Studio Gang and its ongoing quest for further refinement – trying to go smaller, lighter, and with even more delicacy in both early and late-stage design – experimental design, modelling and prototyping go hand-in-hand, leading to exceptional and highly imaginative results.

8–12. Nature Boardwalk, Lincoln Park Zoo, Chicago, IL, 2010.

1–3

3·54

← Techniques
2.1 / p. 23 / Traditional Techniques
2.8 / p. 53 / Virtual Prototyping

GAP Architects [Raymond Lau]

Unfinished and still changeable

Raymond Lau worked on the Galaxy Soho project for Zaha Hadid Architects (ZHA; see page 116) before setting up his own practice in Beijing, GAP. For Lau, prototypes are spatial and performative, although their spatiality can be either virtual or physical. He would not call the mock-ups built for the Galaxy project 'prototypes' because they were intended to demonstrate the quality of construction. The mock-up, for Lau, is a finished thing: 'This is what we can do and this is the best we can do.' A prototype, by contrast, is unfinished and still changeable.

In theory, prototyping is a long process, starting with nothing and repeatedly testing, evaluating and feeding back to create a new version of a design. The prototype will not resemble the finished article at the beginning of the process, but will be close to a true facsimile at the end, with any number of prototypes in-between. Compared to a physical prototype, the digital variety offers the designer more possibilities, and has the potential to provide more information. It can be linked to a database, spreadsheets or parametric formulae, and is much quicker to test. In some ways, the digital prototype has the veracity of the physical kind, but it is not there yet.

For the Galaxy Soho project, there were two rounds of mock-ups. It was a large project, and any problems in one area would have had an impact on many others. For the Sky Soho Leasing Showroom (2013), a smaller job designed by GAP with one-off details, the prototyping had to be incorporated into the construction process on-site. The

1. Sky Soho Leasing Showroom, Beijing, China, 2013: The site of the showroom prior to work starting on the interior.

2. The VIP corridor leading to the showroom was designed parametrically.

3. The complex parts of the project are explained to the workforce on-site.

4–6

7

8–9

showroom's novel design led to a certain amount of trial and error, and to the contractor reworking parts of the design. In effect, it was a case of prototyping *in situ*, with only a small percentage of the prototyping having to be done off-site, in a factory.

Things are changing. The technologies available to the engineering and architectural-manufacturing sectors have caught up with the formal demands of realizing ZHA's architecture over the life of that practice. GAP, by contrast, was born into a culture of digital prototyping and knows nothing else. Digital technology enables the designer to experiment and test their ideas much more easily. It also allows them to develop more challenging designs because the technology is there to realize them.

4. Sky Soho Leasing Showroom: The precast GRG (glass-reinforced gypsum) panels are fixed to the ceiling.

5. A view of the timber frame used to support the ceiling shapes.

6. Plaster-smoothing following the installation of the ceiling panels.

7. Installation of the ceiling shapes.

8–9. Views of the completed showroom.

1–2

3 · 55

MOS Architects [Michael Meredith]

Prototyping seems to come with a lot of architectural selfies along the way

As with many designers, Michael Meredith of MOS Architects sees the prototype primarily as a means of testing an idea, a period of analysis that is increasingly dominating the process by which the New York-based practice designs its installation-scale projects and such smaller-scale objects as tiles and door handles. The distinction between prototyping and making is changing too, as the practice becomes increasingly involved in producing the final object itself, either in the studio or by collaborating directly with small craft operations; it has even found itself creating the production moulds for a ceramicist, instead of entrusting the whole of the job to the craftsperson as it might have done previously. In fact, MOS has found that being more involved in the making stage is a more efficient way of working, with design, making and production all intersecting, partly through the opportunities afforded by the digital revolution. Often, says Meredith, a bespoke element made by the local machine shop will end up being less expensive than a standard manufactured item would have been.

One project that exemplifies MOS's approach is *Majestic*, a temporary cinema installation at the Wexner Center for the Arts in Columbus, Ohio, designed in collaboration with the Slovenian artist Tobias Putrih and made with the help of a small company in Vermont. Meredith suspects that water-jet cutting was more a hobby than a business for the company's owner, but he was nevertheless effective and affordable. The practice found that one of the best decisions it made during the making phase was to move a couple of its staff to Vermont for a fortnight, where

1–2. A custom acoustic tile (bottom) and the mould from which it was made.

3–4. *Majestic*, Wexner Center for the Arts, Columbus, OH, 2010–11.

5–6

7–8

9

178

5–8. Casting resin blocks for Installation
No. 12 (Souvenir Pile), Venice Architecture
Biennale, 2014.

9. Completed resin blocks for Installation
No. 12 (Souvenir Pile), Venice Architecture
Biennale, 2014.

they could tweak the complex design and directly influence the cutting, despite the actual water-jet cutter being quite a primitive machine.

This melding of prototypes and final outcomes brings the issue of tolerances sharply into focus. Any tolerance issues in the assemblies produced by MOS, typically composed of a large quantity of unique components, seem to be amplified by the sheer numbers involved. Scaled prototypes are used to head this problem off, leading to a sequence of photographs being taken as the refinement work proceeds. Meredith claims that these 'architectural selfies' not only inform the design process but also form part of the prototyping.

Looking at the way in which the designers at MOS work, one is left with the impression that the prototypes and final outcomes are merging; indeed, it is equally difficult to distinguish between the prototypes and the mock-ups. Perhaps this is an inherent aspect of an installation: its experimental nature includes some of the attributes of a typical prototype, and is in itself not so different from a mock-up in intention.

In terms of prototyping performance, Meredith offers an interesting perspective. In the latter part of the 2000s, he was of the view that, ultimately, digital prototyping would render architecture as it is traditionally practised obsolete; instead, it would be undertaken on a computer by a different set of specialists. He is now inclined to suspect that the traditional role of the engineer – to calculate – is the more threatened, as designers now have the tools that allow them to calculate in real time. He still

10–11

12–13

14–15

believes that computers will have an even greater presence in architecture, but also that digital fabrication, through enriching the connection between concept and material outcome, has given the architect an enhanced and more sophisticated role.

Another quality that defines MOS Architects is the degree to which art practice is a key part of its repertoire. Meredith describes the office as a junkyard of prototypes – a living repository of ideas in suspension or formation – and not a graveyard. Ultimately, it is the closeness of prototyping to the beating heart of the office that differentiates it from contractors, who would otherwise have a hands-off relationship to the design process were they undertaking all the prototyping. Meredith feels that by keeping the prototyping in-house as much as possible, the practice is able to nurture its instinct to accommodate 'irrational desires', thereby helping to maintain its innate originality.

10–11. Expanding-foam mock-up for Pavilion No. 8 (Droop), competition entry, 2012.

12–13. Custom vase prototype, 2013.

14–15. Custom ceramic tiles, 2013.

Of the various opinions about prototypes shared through these diverse reflections on the subject, perhaps the one that is most often heard is that they test how something is working, not just how it looks. When it comes to machines and machinery, this notion is conceptually clear. But which aspects of the way things work are being tested when prototyping architecture?

In this section, the featured architects reveal some of the ways in which architectural performance is rehearsed. A simulated storm tests the watertightness of inflated cladding panels where they come together in a node at the meeting of three different planes. This is not a building-science exercise to establish standards, but a trial of new or unique component and assembly systems for a specific building as part of the detailed design process.

One design consortium combines an alternative organic and sustainable composite-material system with surface- and air-cleaning coatings and autonomous solar- and piezo-generated power in a demonstration project. It provides art, interest and education while testing cutting-edge technologies for their ability to withstand the elements and possible wider application in architecture.

For one designer, the fitness of a physical prototype lies in the degree to which its performance corresponds with that of its digital progenitor; for another, the value of a digital simulation lies in its proximity to observed and measured physical behaviours. In every case, the prototype represents a valuable opportunity to test some aspect of the interaction between built architecture and the environment.

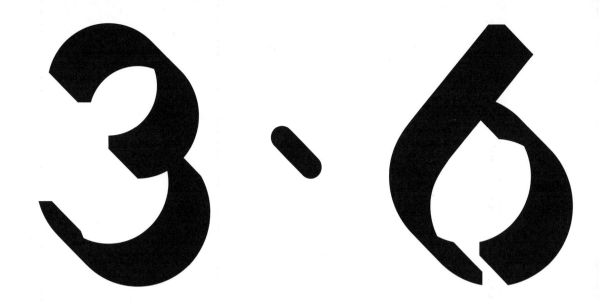

3.6

Testing Performance

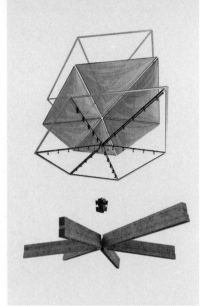

1–2

3·6₁

Foster + Partners

[Jonathan Rabagliati / Ben Scott]

Prototyping as dress rehearsal

1–2. Canary Wharf Crossrail, London, 2015: Computer renderings showing a prototypical component assembly at one node: ETFE cushion, aluminium frame, steel supporting brackets, air pipes, galvanized-steel node and glulam (glued laminated timber) beams.

3 (opposite). Six small ETFE cushions were subjected to rigorous water-tightness tests, using low-pressure water jets (right; see also page 185) and an aircraft propeller to simulate full wind deflection.

Most buildings are built only once and there is only one of them. To borrow an analogy from the world of the theatre, each building is a single performance. With regard to prototyping, Foster + Partners' Jonathan Rabagliati observes that to get this sole performance right, you have to rehearse as much as possible. The Canary Wharf Crossrail project in east London (2015) is a unique project on a unique site with a unique brief, contrasting strongly with existing buildings in Canary Wharf. Prototypes were used by the practice to win the commission – to design a mixed-use scheme above and around the new Canary Wharf Crossrail station – and were part of the process of realization from the pre-tender and tender stages right through to fabrication. A prototype in this context means a physical manifestation of a particular design solution that has not been done before.

Every prototype has a purpose, and it is important to define very clearly what that purpose is. A mock-up is generally made at full size in order to test visual appearance. Moreover, it needs to be done early in the design process, so that there is enough time to change or refine the design in response to any feedback. Mock-ups do not necessarily need to test the materials that have been chosen for the finished building or the construction sequence by which it will be built. A prototype, by contrast, is made with the actual materials and systems to be used for the final design. Even before prototyping in the physical realm, it is important (to continue the earlier analogy) to rehearse as many of the processes,

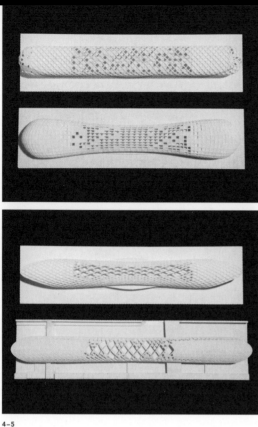

4–5

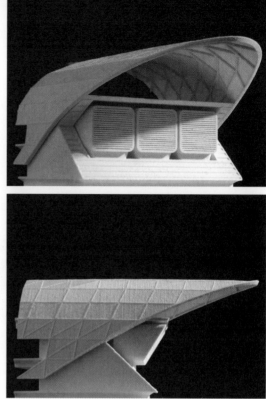

6–7

4–5. Canary Wharf Crossrail: 3D-printed models of proposed roof designs.

6–7. 3D-printed models of cantilever and end buttress used to assess design options and communicate them to the client.

geometries and dependencies as you can – as hard as you can – in the virtual realm. Digital prototyping is also very useful for conducting checks later in the process; in the case of the Crossrail project, digital prototyping was used to check hundreds of unique nodes for any potentially costly clashes (see below). It is generally less expensive to work in 3D digital models and prototypes, but you can only get so far in the digital realm. The materials, assemblies, fabrication techniques and technologies, and their response to different conditions all need to be tested 'in the wild' – through physical prototyping.

Where the design is very novel, tests are necessary to check performance that, in the case of off-the-shelf systems and components, would have already been tested either for or by the manufacturer. With the Crossrail project, the novel use of timber required physical testing to back up the results of analysis. Two Austrian companies were chosen as specialist contractors: Seele for the ETFE cladding, and Wiehag for the timber. Seele had to develop a unique aluminium extrusion for the project in response to the client's desire for a double line of water defence, going beyond a standard ETFE system. The frame comes together in three different planes at each node, creating a potential point of vulnerability.

A first full-scale prototype node with full-scale but downsized ETFE panels was subjected to high-pressure water spray and gale-force winds simulated with a huge industrial propeller. Constructing this prototype

8–9

10–11

12–13

8–9. Canary Wharf Crossrail: Six small ETFE cushions are sprayed with low-pressure water jets as part of the water-tightness test.

10–13. A full-scale mock-up of a single ETFE cushion is used for a number of different tests: water ponding (fig. 10), the reinflation of the cushion after being weighed down by water; sandbagging (fig. 11), designed to simulate snow load; and water run-off (figs 12–13), for assessing gutter-size requirements under heavy rain conditions.

alone was a vital dress rehearsal for the contractor, leading to small changes in the way the flashing was dressed into the outside of the clamping plate, as well as the sequencing of fixing screws. The second mock-up was a single, triangular, aluminium-framed ETFE cushion with rain gutter, which was used for a number of performance tests. The first was the 'sandbagging' test, which simulated a snow load distributed across the whole cushion. The second was an impact test, designed to assess the impact of a large body falling on to the ETFE cushion. The third test recorded the time it took for a cushion to deflate when the air supply was cut off. 'Water ponding' was the fourth test, where the bowl-like space created by the deflated cushion is filled with water to see if, once the air supply has been reconnected, the cushion can be reinflated. Lastly, there were a series of drainage tests to determine the necessary gutter sizes for different cushion angles. A fire engine was brought in to supply the flow rate required to simulate water run-off during heavy rain.

It would have been difficult to determine from calculation alone how water would travel down the ETFE cushions. Would it find its way into the valleys and pond at corners? How should the gutters be sized in different locations? And would the cushions deflate as the water built up, or could the air system reinflate them and push the water off? In each test, the parts that mattered were precisely replicated, from the cushions themselves to the brackets fixing them to the timber frame. Two full-scale prototypes were also built to test the steel nodes connecting the triangular frames,

15–16

17–18

14–15. Canary Wharf Crossrail: First full-scale node prototype using galvanized steel, connecting five glulam beams with steel endplates.

16. Second full-scale node prototype with improved node design. Also being tested here are various cladding options.

17–18. A node is installed on-site. The nodes were bolted to the beams directly, without the use of scaffolding.

with Foster + Partners contributing to the refinement of the node type that Wiehag had proposed at the tender stage.

There are 564 nodes in the roof, which measures 330 metres in length and has a span of 26 metres. Half of these nodes are unique. The nodes selected for prototyping were those that capture most of the different possibilities that can occur at one node. There is a huge amount of variation in the design of the roof, particularly at the cantilevering ends but also in the central section, where there are differently shaped cut-outs over the roof garden below. Some of the openings repeat, others are irregular. The timber depth varies over the length of the building, so the node depths vary too.

On such a bespoke project as this, it is normal for the specialist contractors to build a degree of physical prototyping into their price at tender. The architects include in the tender documents drawings of the prototypes that they consider necessary, and these are reviewed soon after the contract has been assigned. This is the time for a discussion about what it is exactly that is being tested. In the case of the Crossrail project, the winning contractor produced a full-size galvanized-steel node at tender, while each of the four bidding companies produced slightly different samples, including plate connections and flashings. The original design called for the diagonal timbers to twist with the curve of the roof; in the built design, however, the contractor proposed putting that twist into the nodes, rather than the timber, thereby simplifying the design.

19

Large-scale physical prototyping has always been part of Foster + Partners' way of working; for the Hongkong and Shanghai Bank Headquarters in Hong Kong (1986), for example, the mock-ups of the expressed connections in the steel exoskeleton were fabricated with a high level of finish to closely resemble those in the final building. What has changed in the intervening years is the growth of 3D printing and rapid prototyping, which have enabled the designer to create a relatively detailed 3D model of a proposed design early on. This certainly allows for more iterations and greater experimentation. It is also easier for the designer to put forward more options, but more options do not always result in better design. It is necessary to marry lateral exploration of options with vertical exploration of one design in depth: tireless rehearsal for the final performance.

19. Installation of the end ring beam at the west-facing cantilever. The 30-metre-long, doubly curved ring beam is composed of five sections.

1–2

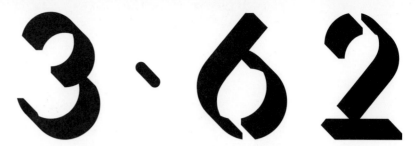

3·62

← Techniques
2.3 / p. 31 / Prototyping Performance
2.8 / p. 53 / Virtual Prototyping

3XN [Kasper Guldager Jensen]

Evaluating the behaviour and performance of objects and processes

For Kasper Guldager Jensen – senior partner at Danish architectural practice 3XN and director of its sustainability research group, GXN – a prototype is a device for evaluating the behaviour and performance of objects and processes. Prototypes may be used to test the functionality of relatively isolated aspects of a design, such as texture, surface quality or the processing of materials. Digital prototypes are able to test the outcome of a sequence of processes in a computer program, the extreme parametric limits of a design or the working range of a parameter value. Prototyping takes the risk out of new ideas and technical innovation. Through involving all parties and stakeholders in this verification process, the experience and knowledge generated in the process of architectural prototyping may also be applied to the development of new products, materials or processes in manufacturing.

The practice's 'Learning from Nature' pavilion at the Louisiana Museum of Modern Art (2009) in Humlebæk, Denmark, exemplifies this commitment to innovation through collaboration. It was the work of a joint venture of twenty different companies, realized over just four months. During this time, conceptualization, design, innovation, material testing and production all had to proceed in parallel, with all parties taking ownership of various aspects of the project.

The pavilion is both a prototype and a demonstrator intended to showcase sustainable 'biological' and 'intelligent' material systems, affirming that such systems can have a legitimate future in the building

1–2. 'Learning from Nature' pavilion, Louisiana Museum of Modern Art, Humlebæk, Denmark, 2009: The design of the pavilion involved the use of physical prototypes, pin-up discussions and digitization. The design itself was optimized to meet the dynamic forces arising from wind load and visitors walking on its surface.

3–4. The pavilion under construction.

7

industry without compromising architectural ingenuity or virtuosity. Biological and reusable materials were substituted for more commonly used synthetic materials. The outer shell, for example, is constructed from a composite of flax fibres in a biological resin based on soya-bean oil and cornflour, regarded as an alternative to glass-fibre-reinforced composites. Sheets of natural cork were used to replace polyethylene foam in the inner core. Addressing the energy needs of the integrated LED lights, 1-millimetre-thick flexible-film solar cells were applied to the doubly curved upper surfaces of the pavilion. These were supplemented by piezoelectric materials in the floor to generate electricity from the footfall of visitors.

The pavilion's surfaces are self-cleaning: a hydrophilic nanostructure disperses rainwater, taking any surface dirt with it. A second coating adds air-cleaning properties: photocatalysis removes up to 70 per cent of pollutants from industrial smog. The pavilion also uses phase-changing material to retain heat. When the temperature falls to a certain level, the liquid material solidifies, releasing energy; as the temperature rises, it liquefies, absorbing energy. It is estimated that this technology will save 10 to 15 per cent of the energy currently used in the heating and cooling of buildings. The pavilion's design is also optimized structurally, with the specification calling for exactly 14 layers of fibre and 84 millimetres of cork to meet the dynamic forces from wind and people walking on its surface. The pavilion thus prototypes a range of new material technologies, as well as breaking ground in the processes used to produce its ambitious form.

5–6. 'Learning from Nature' pavilion: Factory-finishing and installation on-site.

7. The floor of the pavilion uses piezoelectric technology to convert the movement of visitors into electricity, which, in turn, is used to power the pavilion's lighting. Each visitor has the potential to generate 12 watts of power.

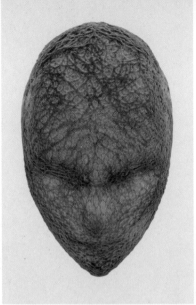

1–2

1–2 & 3 (opposite). Intimacy Mask,
textile prototype, New York, NY, 2015.

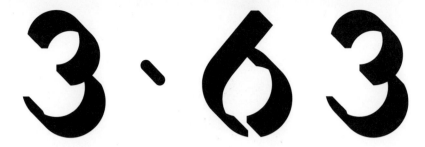

← Techniques
2.6 / p. 45 / Prototyping Through Addition
2.8 / p. 53 / Virtual Prototyping

Francis Bitonti

A piece of the thing that shows the behaviour

New York-based designer Francis Bitonti graduated in architecture after initial excursions into writing, marine biology and fine art with a focus on animation. He has also worked in film post-production. His adaptation to the digital realm is so complete that he never has any issues with the veracity of his 'virtual' creations. The physical prototypes or artefacts that ensue hold no surprises for him. Rather, the challenge for Bitonti is to match the qualities of the digital material, including colour, luminosity and reflectivity, an example being the Squiggle Rack, a bicycle rack created on a computer and subsequently materialized in deep-orange ABS plastic.

Many of Bitonti's designs start life as patterns of numbers without any initial form or shape. Using growth algorithms, he observes the behaviours emerging from the numbers before assigning shape or other attributes. He then visualizes the work using a computer, a process requiring geometry and render settings to give it an initial materiality. (In some ways, the render is the first prototype.) Next comes tactility. Small physical samples provide a sense of the material's flexibility and its response to touch. From there, Bitonti returns to the computer, refining the inputs that have been used to generate the material properties. Bitonti notes how much he enjoys computing, the simple operations that accumulate to produce results way beyond initial expectations.

Bitonti sees his own working methods as a form of simulation, as constant prototyping. There are no models – these, he says, would

6–8

4–5

4–5. Squiggle Rack, New York, NY:
The Squiggle Rack prototype is finished
with automotive paint.

6–8. The completed bicycle rack in use.

9–10

11

12

9. Schistose Mirror: Pattern development.

10. CNC milling of the mirror's surface. The mirror is made from high-density polyurethane foam finished with an automotive paint.

11–12. The completed mirror.

be too removed from materiality. He does foresee a time when digital simulation will be good enough to eliminate physical prototyping. At present, however, this is still some way off. The experience of the novel materials he is creating using contemporary printing technology – materials that, in some cases, are 'more natural than nature' – remains physical and actual. Moreover, clients really need a physical prototype.

Bitonti's physical prototypes are generally just small samples, from which the designer then extrapolates. This way of working is partially a response to the current high cost of some of the production processes he uses, but is also part of his workflow. For example, in order to understand better the parameters with which he is working, Bitonti might order a range of samples to be printed using materials in different combinations. In fact, Bitonti's studio has made a point of exploiting the possibilities inherent in multi-material 3D printing. The materials themselves range from the hard and transparent to the soft and black. Printed from a bitmap rather than a geometrical description, they display gradient shifts from one material to another with hazy intermediate zones. By experimenting with the way in which the filament is laid down and the tooling organized, Bitonti has found that it is possible to obtain dramatically different material properties and cut down on expensive machine time. Currently, the outlets for this inventive design approach are still highly bespoke, but Bitonti sees it as a pathway to the mass- and high-volume custom-production that he believes is not far off.

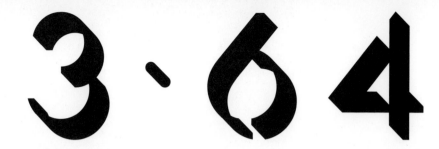

3·64

← Techniques
2.3 / p. 31 / Prototyping Performance
2.7 / p. 49 / Enter the Robot
2.8 / p. 53 / Virtual Prototyping

196

CITA

A probe for material evidence

A prototype is an intermediate step, allowing the designer to move forward; it is 'proto', the first thing, yet prescient of something to come. The Centre for Information Technology in Architecture (CITA) at the Royal Danish Academy of Fine Arts has a threefold strategy towards prototyping. The 'speculative probe' is a poetic, open-ended interrogation of materials or technology. The 'prototype' is the first full-scale test using the actual materials and technology, a means of understanding their behaviour in the context of the design speculations. The 'demonstrator' is also at full scale, but is extended to architectural dimensions, bringing more complex spatial considerations into play. These three kinds of prototype do not always appear in this order. In the case of 'The Rise' (2013), for example – an installation examining the concept of 'growing architecture', created for an exhibition at Espace Fondation EDF in Paris – the team had been engaged in a lot of full-scale prototyping of joints, connections and single elements. They found, however, that they needed to return to the more conceptual speculative probe, making a small and beautiful model that clarified the original idea and inspired them to continue with the 1:1 prototyping.

At CITA, despite the focus on information technology, prototyping always includes physical testing at full scale because the centre's practice is materials-based. But because its area of interest is architecture, the prototype is never the whole of the design; rather, it is always more of a demonstrator. In other, non-architectural contexts, such as software

1–2. 'The Rise', *Alive: Designing with Living Systems,* Espace Fondation EDF, Paris, France, 2013: Installation views.

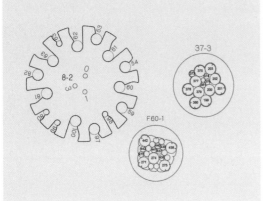

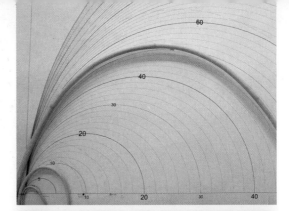

3–4

5–6

3. 'The Rise': Member continuity through multiple connection nodes, as demonstrated by identifying all members that pass through node no. 6.

4. Sample drawings of various star and packing nodes. From left: star node, 'tight' packing node and 'loose' packing node for the connection of a strut to a flower.

5. Identification of minimum bending radius by rattan section.

6. A star node. Each piece of rattan is labelled, identifying its corresponding node, location and strand strength.

7. Installation view, Espace Fondation EDF, Paris, 2013.

8. Packing node and star connection system in the finished installation.

design, the approach to prototyping is very different. CITA's Martin Tamke says that software designers 'really know what a prototype is and they are afraid of it because it has to show that everything works – it is the decisive step into big production. The software prototype is almost complete.' By contrast, an architectural prototype is a validation of process and thinking. This idea of validation is fundamental. A building itself is a great prototype as long as there is sufficient evaluation. In Tamke's view, while there is far more evaluation of completed buildings than before, it is still generally insufficient. Digital prototyping is important, cost-effective and provides lots of new information. But it has to be validated and based on empirical data and other prototypes; in other words, you have to be able to evaluate at least part of the digital prototype with physical tests. The digital simulation of the energy behaviour of buildings in Denmark as the basis for design approval, for example, needs to be matched by the measurement and evaluation of the buildings, both completed and in use, in order to re-inform the digital modelling.

CITA's work is all about the friction between the digital and the material – a productive friction that defines the creative space. The full-scale physical demonstrator also serves as a vital 'gathering point' for designers and researchers, a means of collaborating with a lot of people at once and getting instant feedback as to the accuracy of your assumptions, rather than waiting for the evidence. It is also a powerful tool for capturing the imagination of practice and industry partners.

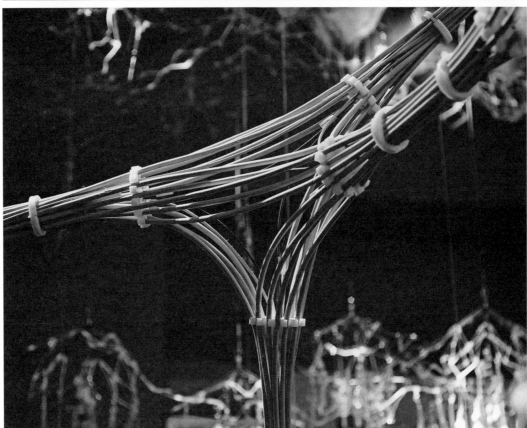

7–8

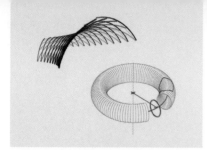

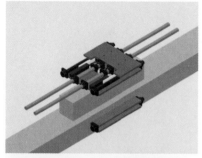

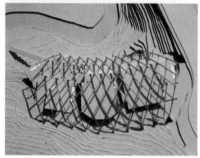

1–3

3.65

Architecture Workshop [Christopher Kelly]

There is nothing more effective than leaving a physical model or a prototype on someone's desk

1. Waitomo Glowworm Caves Visitor Centre, Waitomo, New Zealand, 2014: Digital prototype of toroidal geometry, prepared by Architecture Workshop for structural engineers Dunning Thornton.

2. Digital prototype of second iteration of LVL (laminated veneer lumber) joint in glulam arch, developed in conversation with the subcontractor and builder after a site inspection of the full-scale prototype (see fig. 6).

3. The first model of the canopy, showing the idea in context, made by Architecture Workshop for a presentation to the client.

4. A full-scale foam-board mock-up of an LVL rib crossover, made by Architecture Workshop.

Christopher Kelly is the founding principal of Architecture Workshop, an architectural practice based in Wellington, New Zealand. His work is a savvy fusion of lessons learnt from his lengthy apprenticeship at Renzo Piano's studio in Genoa, Italy. Architecture Workshop deploys a full measure of what is known locally at least as 'Kiwi ingenuity'. Prototyping for Kelly is simply the pathway to realizing the final building, which in his view is itself a full-scale prototype. The prototype is also a key element of the design service that the practice offers its clients – a '3D study piece'.

To Architecture Workshop, the differences between models, mock-ups and prototypes are clear. Models for the practice are scaled representations, whereas prototypes need to be full-scale. The practice regards the making of prototypes as the traditional method by which the architect liaises with the builder over the optimal route for getting from the design to the built outcome. The prototype, in its view, has to be a working version of what is proposed; that is to say, it needs to perform as if it were part of the completed building, revealing the viability of hinges, joints, and so on. The mock-up, in contrast, can be made from any material suitable for the task, such as painted MDF, and is designed to simulate what the design will look like at full scale.

In practice, however, Kelly has found that getting contractors to see the full value of a prototype can be difficult. In his experience, the contractor will often make the prototype off-site simply to understand for themselves what is involved. Kelly's preference is always for the

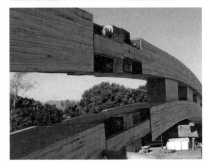

4–6

7–8

5. Waitomo Glowworm Caves Visitor Centre: A prototype of an LVL rib segment is tested in a jig. Note the twist and radius formers, and the measurement of 'relaxation' when the rib is released from the jig. On the basis of this observation, the design team recalculated the digital geometry model.

6. Prototyping the assembly. The intention behind the design of the first version of the splice joint was *not* to create a clumsy silhouette. The contractor also had problems joining rib segments together and bolting the joint.

7. Two arch segments with a single crossover and typical cladding support are prepared for inspection in the yard of Hawkins Construction.

8. LVL rib segments are laid up on-site after the prototyping process.

9

10–11

9. Waitomo Glowworm Cave Visitors
Centre: The view along the dining level
towards the exit from the cave. Note the
positions of the splice joints, as developed
during the prototyping phase.

10–11. Views of the ETFE cladding.

12 (opposite). A view of the completed
roof structure showing examples of the
crossovers and splice joints.

prototype to be made on-site using the subcontractors involved in the
actual building. In this way, the prototype can be a learning aid for the
whole team as it develops its strategies for how best to proceed with what
is typically an innovative design. Frustratingly, he observes, this can be
the case even when the intention is to incorporate the prototype into the
completed building – that is, at very little extra cost to the project.

In terms of billing clients for prototypes, Kelly prefers to absorb the
cost into the practice's fee. The timber canopy for the Waitomo Glowworm
Caves Visitor Centre (2010), for example, required the substantial testing
of prototypes in a wind tunnel – something that was well beyond the ken
of the client. Conversely, in the case of the contractor, Kelly encourages
them to produce prototypes at their own expense, persuading them of the
longer-term cost benefits of ironing-out potential complexities well before
the critical phase of a project. Kelly finds that contractors will routinely
produce something between a rough model and a basic prototype on their
own initiative in order to understand, for example, unfamiliar geometries.
Such an object is not really a prototype, he notes, but 'physical modeling'.

Ultimately, the practice uses prototypes to test, and subsequently
refine, a physical rather than a spatial outcome. They are almost always
preceded by a scale model for the client, and sometimes one for the
builder. Kelly claims that, despite the marvels of digital prototyping, nothing
is more effective than leaving a model on someone's desk as a follow-up
to a conversation.

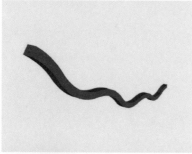

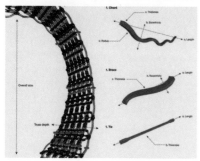

1–3

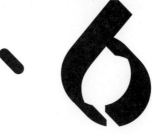

3 · 66

← Techniques
2.3 / p. 31 / Prototyping Performance
2.7 / p. 49 / Enter the Robot
2.8 / p. 53 / Virtual Prototyping

AL_A [Maximiliano Arrocet]

Testing the limits

Maximiliano Arrocet, director at AL_A, expects prototypes to fail in some way, especially as they are often used by the London-based practice to explore fabrication techniques that are not necessarily native to architecture. Prototypes give the designer an idea of the limits of using a particular material or technology in a novel or risky way. Consequently, prototyping generally happens early in the design process, to determine whether to pursue a radical idea or revert to something safer. In less risky projects, such as a façade design for which the designer is confident of finding a good solution but not yet sure of the best way to achieve it, they can also be used later in the process.

Prototypes do not necessarily need to look like the final product; rather, they are used strategically to test the specific attributes of a design. Some prototypes are used to explore buildability – for instance, the best way of fixing an exterior panel by hand, from the back. Such a prototype would likely come late in the design process, and be financed by the client. By contrast, earlier, in-house experimental prototypes test an experience: what does a structure of thin carbon tubes oscillating by 10 centimetres really look or feel like, or what is it like to experience a certain level of sound? Perception does not always conform to centimetres and decibels, even if these can be accurately calculated and predicted.

Prototypes can also be digital. A good example of the use of such prototypes as part of the design process is *Timber Wave*, an installation for the Victoria and Albert Museum in London, designed by AL_A in

1. *Timber Wave*, Victoria and Albert Museum, London, 2011: The curved chord elements were built up from thin layers of glued laminated timber.

2. The installation was composed of fourteen types of chord element, ranging from 2.6 to 4.6 metres in length.

3. Bespoke scripting produced highly accurate and changeable models.

4–5. The three-storey-high structure reflected the grand proportions of the museum's Cromwell Road entrance.

6–7

8–9

10–11

6–15. Spencer Dock Bridge, Dublin, Ireland, 2009: CNC milling of the formwork, and the formwork *in situ*.

collaboration with Arup as part of the 2011 London Design Festival. A modelling program was used to generate different geometrical solutions. These were then analysed structurally, with the results feeding back into the geometrical model in order to find the optimal solution. If AL_A had not had the opportunity to analyse hundreds, even thousands, of possible solutions, the individual elements of the installation would have been a lot thicker and less delicate, and the practice would not have had the confidence to choose a fine-boned aesthetic and say to Arup, 'Let's go for this one'.

The brief for the installation, commissioned by the American Hardwood Export Council, was to build something using the timber in its catalogue – much of which was not best suited to outdoor structural use. In creating *Timber Wave*, the architects designed a truss system, keeping costs down through the use of small pieces of timber assembled into modules: S-shaped assemblies of chords and braces. Arup identified where the twist in the structure resulted in areas of maximum eccentricity, which concentrated the stresses, and recommended the limited use of steel plates internally. The differential strength of the wood along and across the grain led to cross-lamination. Working with expert joiners Cowley Timberwork, the designers also experimented with small physical prototypes of segments of the structure, testing joints and the suitability of various laminate glues. But the key prototyping was digital, communicated through Excel spreadsheets exchanged with the engineers.

12–13

14–15

16–17

It is unlikely that digital prototypes will replace the physical kind altogether. For his part, Arrocet believes that, although they are very useful for testing a large number of options, they give the designer too much control. With the digital prototype, such as a computer rendering, the environmental conditions are perfect. What you really want, however, is to test things in all conditions – on every day of the year – for weathering, tactility and buildability. And these, of course, are physical phenomena.

The Spencer Dock Bridge in Dublin (2009) was very much driven by physical prototyping. The first prototype was a large polystyrene bench cut from a digital file using a robotic arm. It was instrumental in shifting the perspective of the building contractor and bringing the project in on budget. When AL_A's design was first presented, the timber formwork that would have been needed to realize the complex geometries was going to cost more than the bridge itself. But the idea of using milled polystyrene-foam blocks for the non-structural components of the bridge, choosing an appropriate density of foam and protecting and strengthening it with three coats of polyuria, saved the day. Adopting an approach common in the shipbuilding industry worked well for everyone: the contractor was able to control the cost, and the architect the shape.

In both the *Timber Wave* and the Dublin bridge project, prototyping was critical and successful. The architects handed over 3D digital files directly for construction, bypassing the need for shop drawings.

16–17. Spencer Dock Bridge: Views of the completed bridge.

3 · 67

Eva Jiricna

A fully operational object

To the Czech-born architect Eva Jiricna, founder of London-based Eva Jiricna Architects (EJA), a prototype is a fully operational, full-scale object that shows how the final project is going to work, perform and behave. Anything less, and it's a mock-up. For this exacting and experienced designer, a prototype is something you have to hold in your hands and experience physically. The expression 'digital prototype' does not resonate with Jiricna because you cannot fully test a digital representation, no matter how convincing or valuable it is visually. 'The detail', she says, 'is extremely important because this is actually what we live with.' She also notes that while the prototype is the first cost to be dropped by those inexperienced in using them, anyone who has worked with the prototype before – client or contractor – wants to do so again.

Having been taught by an older generation of architects with a functional focus, for whom prototyping and testing were central to understanding new materials in architecture between the world wars, Jiricna believes that, in general, there is probably less prototyping and less interest in really good detailing in contemporary architectural practice. The technical competence and experience is now often left to the manufacturers. EJA tries to incorporate prototyping into every single job 'because there is always something you can spot on a prototype which otherwise could cause a massive amount of problems later on'.

The practice's staircase in the west wing of Somerset House in London, inspired by William Chambers' Nelson Staircase in the east wing

1-3. Staircase for the west wing of Somerset House, London, 2013: Fabricating the mould for the landing sections.

4–6

7–8

9–10

4–6. Somerset House staircase:
Completing the mould for the landing
sections; pouring a landing section using
Ductal; and removing the cast landing
section from the mould.

7–8. The mould for a step in fabrication,
and pouring a step into the completed mould.

9–10. A step is removed from the mould
and then finished.

and completed in 2013, is a bold spiral staircase composed of cantilevered treads extending from a lightweight, fine-steel-mesh tower linking the four floors of the Grade 1-listed building. In lieu of the vagaries of stone, the staircase uses Ductal, a dense, ultra-strong, non-porous type of concrete used for underwater construction, allowing the treads, which support one another, to be slender and shapely as well as hard-wearing. A series of prototypes encouraged the practice to proceed with the design, as the engineer's calculations were unable to prove conclusively that the bearing of each step on the next was sufficient. Following completion of the second prototype, the amount of material in each tread was reduced, making the shape more elegant, and curving and softening the potentially brittle edges. The third prototype tested the connections between treads and between one of the landings and the central tower. This revealed a little more movement than expected, but once these structural issues had been resolved the staircase went into production. The treads were cast in Italy with reusable moulds and organic-fibre reinforcement. Once cast, the treads were polished, the joints tested and the top surface given a texture.

Other staircases by EJA include a staircase for the jewelry gallery at the Victoria and Albert Museum in London (2008) and, at the time of writing, an unbuilt staircase for a new gallery at the New-York Historical Society, using glass as the primary structure. The latter will require fundamental prototyping and testing to understand the real elasticity and limits of glass in this radical application.

13

14

Like the Lloyd's building in London (1986) – Jiricna's first experience of large-scale prototyping while working in the office of Richard Rogers – EJA's challenging, elliptical concert hall for the Cultural Centre in the city of Zlin (2011) required the production of a large number of complex prototypes in order to refine and validate the design before construction. Unlike Lloyd's, however, there was so little money in the budget that the designers could not afford to make a mistake. For the Cultural Centre, the first such centre to be built in the Czech Republic since the Second World War, eighty mock-ups were needed before a 10-metre-square prototype of the white, textured-concrete acoustic panels could be sent for laboratory testing. The fabricators of the prototype produced three versions free of charge, and the Czech Technical University in Prague helped with the testing. The exterior glass-brick walls also required prototyping in order to test the application of a new Swedish system of tape between the bricks. The absolutely rigid budget (60 per cent European money for the city's first cultural building, and 40 per cent city money) necessitated scrupulous testing and the almost exclusive use of local fabricators and suppliers, many of which were very generous and enthusiastic in their support for the project.

11–14. Somerset House staircase:
Views of the completed staircase.

Given that digital design is essentially data-related, it is possible to point to a bilateral relationship between data and design: the latter leading to the production of useful data that is highly relevant to the whole process and, conversely, the former being used to steer the design. This section includes several examples of this relationship, as well as instances where the prototype gives form to the invisible world of data not as a physical outcome, but rather as a powerful driver intended to get the best from the often multidisciplinary design team, as in the example of CASE RPI and aspects of SUPERSPACE.

The ongoing work at the Sagrada Família in Barcelona showcases the production of 1:1 prototypes using highly sophisticated data streams – in this case, those emanating from the essentially geometrical constructs that are the basis of Gaudí's 'codex' of doubly ruled surfaces. Such examples are clear manifestations of the possibilities of 'file to factory' data streaming: the sending of data from the digital model directly to the machinery used to produce the physical prototypes and, ultimately, the building itself.

Other examples in this section include the work of Franken\ Architekten and the ICD in Stuttgart, where the protagonists make a link between data, the algorithm and production. In such cases, there is the possibility of completely decoupling architectural design from all that might be regarded as 'traditional practice'. While this is not explicitly stated nor implied in this section, suffice it to say that the projects offer an insight into the cleanness of such a direct link between design, data and digital production. Prototypes emerge from the design and making processes that can be managed entirely as virtual manifestations of underlying data.

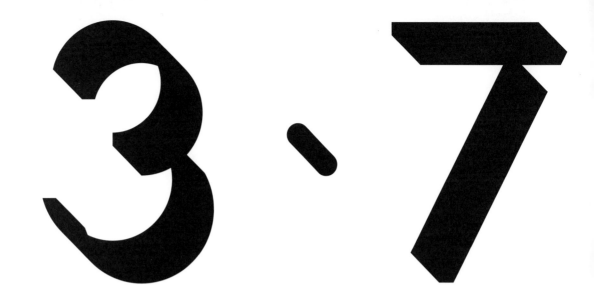

3.7

Manifestation of Data

1–3

3·71

← Techniques
2.4 / p. 37 / CNC Revolution
2.8 / p. 53 / Virtual Prototyping

Franken\Architekten

Protoype as manifestation of data

German architectural practice Franken\Architekten sees data as being at the core of any project. Even the architectural geometry is a data set, one that holds the key to the design and may lead to multiple derivations. A prototype is a piece of one such derivation that is used to test and validate assumptions. These assumptions might relate to the structural performance of the design, its optical properties or even its behaviour.

One Franken\Architekten project to which optics were central was Home Couture (2005), the first flagship store for the exclusive tiles, fittings and bathroom accessories produced by building-materials company Raab Karcher. A special type of glass was developed for the street façade, incorporating a series of optical effects similar to looking at something on the bottom of a swimming pool. As one walks past the store and looks through the windows, the changing optics produce distortions of the objects within. These effects were prototyped using digital simulations, as well as physical samples of the milled acrylic glass. The design celebrates a kind of *flâneur* approach to the relationship between store and street.

Another example of the practice's approach to prototyping – in which data is manifest in a very physical way – is Kleine Rittergasse 11 (2014), a three-storey property in Frankfurt. The project is part of the renewal of the city's old quarter, Alt-Sachsenhausen, the unique character of which developers are attempting to both preserve and reflect through a combination of housing and small-scale commerce. Franken\Architekten was commissioned to create a mixed-use space incorporating a photo

1–3. Home Couture, Berlin, Germany, 2005: CNC fabrication of the windows for the street façade. Variations in the windows produce optical effects similar to looking at objects at the bottom of a swimming pool.

4 (opposite). Interior view of the completed showroom.

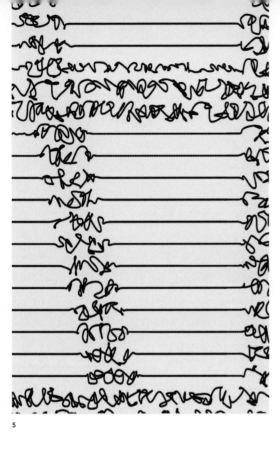

5

6–7

studio, office and apartments. Although the original, war-damaged house on the site had to be demolished, the practice looked for a way of commemorating what had gone before in the new building.

The design of the building adopts the three-storey, gabled-roofed profile of the traditional, half-timbered houses in the area. The base of the property has been covered in natural stone, while the plastered upper stories have been finished with a sheet material, a type of stone foam. The timber framing of the original house has been invoked by means of a pattern milled into the sheet material where the frame would have once been visible. The milling follows a randomized path or 'jitter', generated and controlled algorithmically to create a subtle evocation of the original timber frame, as seen at different times of the day.

Iterative physical prototyping was key to refining the form of the jitter, the depth of the milling head and the effect of seeing the jitter in different lighting conditions. The milling machine used for the project was owned by the client, thereby facilitating a collaborative approach towards iterative testing.

5. Kleine Rittergasse 11, Frankfurt, Germany, 2014: Concept sketch for the façade pattern.

6. A view of the original building that occupied the site.

7. A computer rendering of the new building.

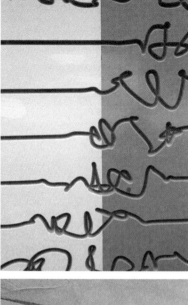

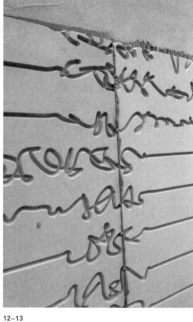

8–13. Kleine Rittergasse 11: Prototypes and trial assembly of the façade.

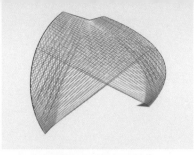

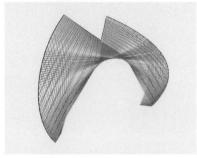

1–3

← Techniques
2.3 / p. 31 / Prototyping Performance
2.7 / p. 49 / Enter the Robot
2.8 / p. 53 / Virtual Prototyping

ICD [Achim Menges]

Protoyping the process – algorithmic and making

1–2. ICD/ITKE Research Pavilion, University of Stuttgart, Germany, 2012: A prerequisite for the design, development and realization of the project was a closed, digital-information chain linking the project's model, finite element simulations, material testing and robot control. Form-finding and material and structural design were directly integrated into the design process.

3. An illustration showing the tool path and winding sequence for the construction of the pavilion.

4–5. The fabrication of the pavilion was performed on-site in a purpose-built, weatherproof manufacturing environment by a six-axis robot coupled with an external seventh axis in the form of a turntable. Located on a 2-metre-high pedestal, and with an overall working span of 4 metres, the robot placed the fibres on a temporary steel frame, which was moved in a circular motion by the robotically controlled turntable.

For Achim Menges, founding director of the Institute for Computational Design (ICD) in Stuttgart, prototyping in architecture has moved away from testing particular objects or material configurations, and is focusing instead on processes, including the tools and algorithms underlying the generation of form and performance. He talks about a shift towards 'prototypical improvisations' – ways of making things that mirror the shift from descriptive geometry to a more computationally based process. To Menges, the physical mock-up more closely resembles the way something is intended to be, based on an explicit systems logic, while the prototype rehearses the processes to be used in its making, based on coded or embedded implicit knowledge. At the same time, clients are increasingly expecting to receive a prototype that closely resembles the final outcome: there is less inclination to grapple with abstractions.

Leaving behind standard solutions and seeking unique, project-specific ones increases the need for physical prototyping in architecture, in order to establish how a new system will play out in the material world. This represents a break from a typological, rule-of-thumb or experience-based approach. At the ICD, prototyping has changed in response to the changing scale of its projects, from product design to small- and medium-sized buildings. In the case of industrial or product design, something can be prototyped in its entirety. At the architectural scale, by contrast, the comprehensive prototype is impossible, so there is a greater emphasis on testing critical parameters and more focus on the processes of design

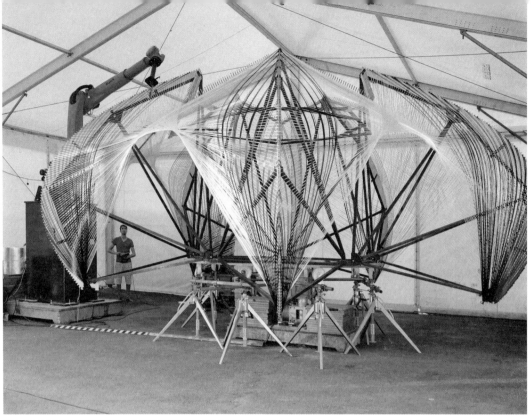

4–5

6–7

8

and production. The ICD's approach is to keep physical prototyping and computational simulation intertwined in the form of a 'physical computational' process.

Menges observes how manufacturing has become more and more like prototyping. Emblematic of this shift is the way in which rapid prototyping has quickly become a form of manufacturing. He believes that once we have absorbed the paradigm shift of computation infusing fabrication as well as design, prototyping, as it is traditionally understood, will become obsolete. All industries appear to be moving towards much more individualized output: production on a more regional basis, new ways of introducing difference, items within a product range fully differentiated from each other. In this context, the prototype is all about commonalities or system rules.

The small-scale model of the ICD's Research Pavilion (2012) currently on display at the institute is actually a prototype of the fibre-winding process used for the final structure. It was originally intended to be a scale model for exhibition, but the process of making provided a large amount of information about the winding procedure and the interaction between the different layers of the winding. Indeed, it was created in exactly the same way as the pavilion proper – only the number of fibres and material used ended up being different – making the model a prototype of the construction sequence. By using the intended building methods for the modelling process, the designer enters a grey zone between modelling and prototyping and, as a result, learns a great deal.

6–8. ICD/ITKE Research Pavilion:
Details of the completed pavilion.

9–10. The completed pavilion *in situ*.

1–4

1–4. Smart Solutions for Spatial Planning, London, 2008: Four stages from a massing-generation prototype that correlated network performances to street sections and eventually envelopes. The prototype was an integrated model that was abandoned in favour of an open framework in order to allow design heuristics to drive the individual stages, rather than letting the algorithms determine design solutions.

3·73

← Techniques
2.3 / p. 31 / Prototyping Performance
2.8 / p. 53 / Virtual Prototyping

SUPERSPACE [Christian Derix]

Experiential prototypes of archetypes of use

The prototypes produced by SUPERSPACE – formerly the Computational Design and Research group at Aedas, now the research arm of international design firm Woods Bagot – are not versions of an outcome of the design process, nor mock-ups of part of a design created to test its performance in real conditions. They are not, in other words, meant to be the real thing. Rather, they are intended to test the user's experience or a design heuristic in a virtual environment, and their success is measured by the extent to which they change perception, behaviour and the design process. This approach to prototyping is exemplified by three of the research group's projects: Smart Solutions for Spatial Planning (SSSP), a model for designing sustainable neighbourhoods; a model for user-centred visual perception in virtual architecture; and the VITA shelving system, based initially on a cellular automaton and subsequently on a maze-building algorithm better suited to generating continuous shelving patterns. This last project included a participatory, web-based design interface, or 'configurator', for clients.

The SSSP was prototyped by applying it to different design cases with different user groups. While the core of the model can be retained and reapplied in different urban and building projects, much of it has to be adapted to each new design scenario. As such, it was the overall 'system' of modelling that was being prototyped. The prototype model was regarded as a success if the person driving it, the designer or user, understood the process embodied in the model and could see a different

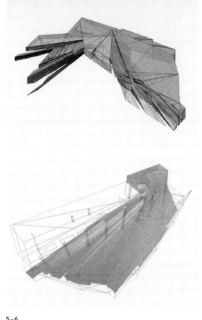

5–6

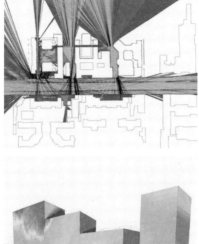

7–8

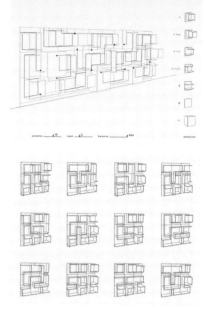

9–10

5–6. National September 11 Memorial, New York, NY, 2007: Two digital representations of visibility conditions at the memorial.

7. An exercise in the evaluation of 'surprise' conducted by students at Milan Politecnico in 2014 using the SUPERSPACE Dynamic Isovist program.

8. The visual impact of proposed massing at Euston Square, London, 2013.

9–10. VITA shelving system, Milan, 2008: Designed for MDF Italia, the online system allows clients to configure their own modular shelving units.

quality to their design as a result of using it. For SUPERSPACE, the value of prototyping in this way lies in the observation of the unfolding of process through exploration within an interactive model that already has the compliance constraints, or generative system, on board. The designer or stakeholder can explore possible solutions that meet the criteria in a live, interactive-feedback environment.

SUPERSPACE's Christian Derix worked with Paul Coates at the University of East London in research projects exploring how certain algorithms worked and their potential. He saw an opportunity to introduce prototypical behavioural processes into real-world design projects, starting with the design of a new school. The requirements for the school were no more than 5 minutes changeover time between any pair of classrooms, even quicker emergency egress times, certain combinations of room types and areas in proximity to one another, and particular visibility standards for signage and wayfinding. These were examples of measurables that could be included in the model. Designers of the computational model, with their expert understanding of the criteria they were working with, were able to interact with the model. By altering the inputs, they could provide feedback on the effect of changes – a form of virtual prototyping. This became the basis for a series of models for different building projects and, ultimately, an understanding of the underlying generics of a spatial planning system. One generalized model has now resulted from about seven years of testing different versions on different projects.

1–2

3·74

Jordi Faulí

[Architect Director, Sagrada Família]

Prototypes provide the fundamental route to decision-making

1. Sagrada Família, Barcelona, Spain, 1882–: A full-scale prototype/mock-up for part of the ceiling vaults over the nave crossing.

2. Crossing ceiling vaults under construction (2008).

3 (opposite). A full-size ceiling-vault prototype is hoisted into position for evaluation purposes.

The Catalan architect Antoni Gaudí (1852–1926) is remembered, among other things, for the close interest he took in the realization of his designs. The son of a kettle maker, his ability to pick up the tools of a blacksmith and demonstrate the artistic effect he wanted to achieve, for example, has been widely commented on. It could be argued that, for Gaudí, the building process was part of the design process, and that his participation in both was essentially an act of prototyping. Gaudí, of course, was a highly creative and original individual, and we might regard his approach to prototyping in architecture as unique. Are there any important differences for his successors, who are deeply enmeshed in today's digital design and fabrication environment?

At the Sagrada Família (1882–), Gaudí's great, unfinished church in Barcelona, the post of architect director was taken up by Jordi Faulí in 2012. Like his predecessor, Jordi Bonet, he insists on absorbing all that is known about Gaudí's modus operandi as part of the challenge of advancing the project towards its expected completion in 2026. Faulí's team is based on-site in a studio only metres away from where Gaudí himself once worked. While the use of aeronautical software and the latest advances in robotic fabrication and stone-cutting would seem to separate current practice from Gaudí's own, there are in fact many similarities between the two. Where Gaudí sculpted by hand in a geometrically rigorous fashion, the present Sagrada Família team has pioneered a form of digital sculpting that mimics closely the way stonemasons work.

4

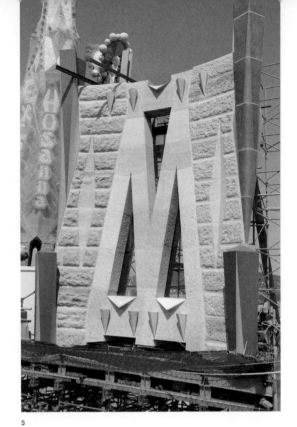

5

4–5. Sagrada Família, 2013: A full-scale prototype of a section of the future central tower under evaluation for colour, texture and shadow at its intended height.

6–7. Sagrada Família, 2006: Full-scale prototype columns for the proposed narthex colonnade in position. The prototypes are made from painted, machine-cut expanded polyurethane.

The question of whether contemporary on-site prototyping has taken on a new meaning since Gaudí's time is a moot point; as far as the current design team is concerned, part of Gaudí's legacy has been to maintain the way the building has been designed through prototyping. As Faulí puts it, prototypes provide the fundamental route to decision-making: the workflows are essentially the same. While there is little likelihood of the present design team picking up the forger's hammer and tongs, they are just as connected to the construction process as Gaudí had been through their intimate knowledge of and participation in the digital fabrication environment. Each member of the team works hand-in-glove with the on-site builders and off-site fabricators.

At the Sagrada Família, the prototype is treated as a sample of the building and, where possible, is made from the materials being used for its construction. Otherwise, it would be seen as a model, which for this project simply serves the role of providing a spatial representation. Prototypes, by contrast, need to be full-scale in order to test appearance, materials, light effects, the joints between materials, textures, colours and constructability. If practicable, prototypes are always tested in their intended location; at the time of writing, for example, large sections of the central towers had been placed in situ at a height of 85 metres from street level for this very purpose. In a project such as this, where every component is likely to be unfamiliar in both composition and appearance, the indispensability of prototyping almost goes without saying.

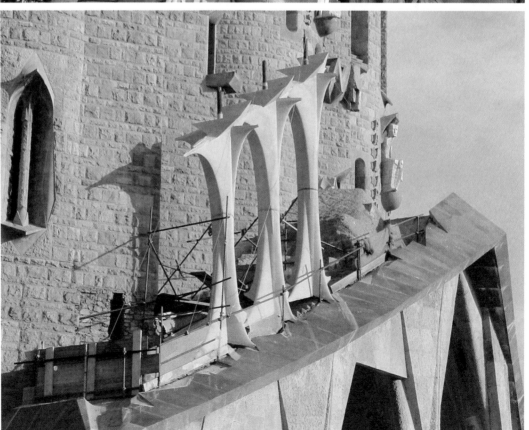

3·75

← Techniques
2.2 / p. 27 / Mock-ups
2.3 / p. 31 / Prototyping Performance
2.4 / p. 37 / CNC Revolution

1–2

1. Integrated Concentrating Solar Façade (ICSF), CASE RPI, New York, NY, 2005–: An early prototype of the ICSF (2007).

2. Prototype installed at the Syracuse University Center of Excellence for operational, performance, and daylighting experimentation.

CASE RPI [Anna Dyson]

Almost all of our prototypes go through testing protocols

According to its website, the Center for Architecture Science and Ecology (CASE) is 'addressing the need for accelerated innovation of built ecologies through the development of next-generation building systems'. Co-hosted by Rensselaer Polytechnic Institute (RPI) and Skidmore, Owings & Merrill (SOM), CASE is a multi-institutional research centre that bridges the gap between the university and practice to form a unique facility in the heart of New York City. Physically independent of both hosts, the centre feels more like an independent laboratory and, on entering the facility, the visitor is greeted by a tremendous sense of active experimentation, with an abundance of fascinating, working prototypes on display.

At the heart of CASE's work is the urgent need to address future cities' demand for water, energy and other resources. The technologies on which it is focused are therefore aimed at locally harnessing ecologically sustainable energy and improving the interaction between human systems and those in the natural world.

The motivation for establishing CASE as a research lab based partly on practice and partly on academia was to get the best from the applied research environment offered by a practice with the scale and history of SOM and, at the same time, bring the next generation of researchers through RPI and its advanced-degree programme in built ecologies. In particular, CASE uses an interdisciplinary approach to facilitate the coming together of architectural and engineering practices, other research institutions, manufacturers and related consultants, all of which are striving

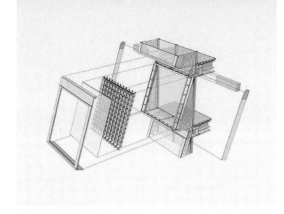

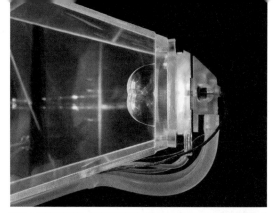

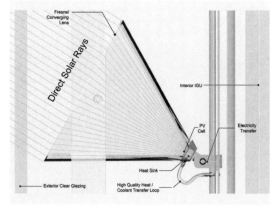

3–4

5–6

3. Integrated Concentrating Solar Façade (ICSF).

4. Section view of an ICSF module showing solar concentration and components.

5. A receiver assembly during solar tracking, including secondary optical element, multi-junction solar cell and water-cooled heat sink.

6. Proposal for retrofitting an ICSF curtain-wall unit into an existing building façade.

for the same thing: performance-driven building technologies that offer a cleaner and self-sustaining built environment.

The link to RPI is a fortuitous one as, from CASE's perspective, the institution has a 'visionary administration', offering an intellectually wide-ranging and rigorous collaborative environment. In working within a transdisciplinary (as opposed to cross-, inter- or multidisciplinary) framework, the contributing disciplines do not become subsumed in the scientifically creative team. CASE's distinctive methodology, combined with the in-between status of being a university-practice, has been contrived deliberately to ensure that academics can still have their contributions recognized within their disciplines and not feel as though their endeavours are moving them away from any tenure-track priorities. For the practices and industries involved, the research environment offers an entrepreneurial workspace with the potential for spin-offs. This is not a done deal, however: CASE maintains an internal discussion questioning the extent to which the team should be developing new knowledge as opposed to new research frameworks.

As the work at CASE is grounded in both biophysics and the physics of energy, prototypes for the centre are usually conceived in relation to physical behaviours – a test of protocols on the pathway to invention. There is also a strong sense that, as a deeply committed research partnership, CASE is, in itself, an ongoing prototype for academy–practice–industry hook-ups offering codependence without any loss of independence.

The word 'progenitor' suggests a seed of something that has a future development trajectory to follow, an original that has the capacity to evolve beyond its basic function as a model. The progenitor, in other words, is the predecessor of an emerging lineage – the precursor to a series of iterative refinements. Specifically raised by Alvise Simondetti of Arup in a discussion on how best to situate the notion of the prototype within the design process, the prototype as progenitor is clearly seen by many as significant within their creative approach, as the following examples demonstrate.

Whereas others introduce the prototype into their design work downstream, once they have a sense of where the project is going, those favouring the progenitor approach feel the need to test specific aspects of the developing design at the very beginning of the process. Such architects as Tim Black of BKK use the prototype to probe the potential viability of an idea. Bob Sheil prototypes in order to take on the unknown, and sees the progenitor approach as a means of breaking new ground. Greg Lynn, too, prototypes to test an emerging concept, whenever introducing anything new or unfamiliar into his practice.

The use of a prototype to tease out a seed of an idea is not a casual or directionless procedure. It is as highly disciplined as the invocation of prototyping at a later stage for the purposes of testing a range of viabilities, such as those of a technical, financial or constructional nature. Progenitorial prototyping may well be a more open-ended approach than the deployment of prototypes to prove physical capabilities, for example, but as a means of discovering fresh design potential, it has plenty of champions.

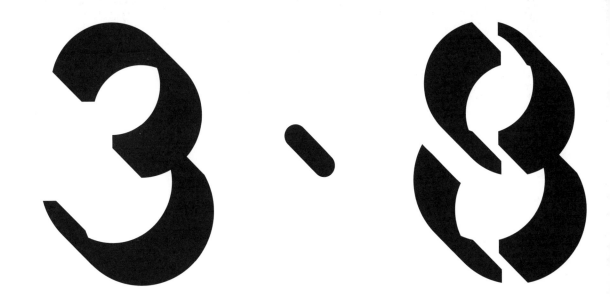

Progenitor

1–3

3·81

← Techniques
2.2 / p. 27 / Mock-ups
2.8 / p. 53 / Virtual Prototyping

Arup [Alvise Simondetti]

Foresight

1–3. Digital environments for experiential design, enhancing designers' perception, 2010–12: Screen grabs from the three horizontal monitors of the designer's viewing facility showing station signage. The avatar figures are dynamic and move around the scene to create a realistic environment.

4. Currently being developed at the University of Warwick, this equipment will enable designers to 'smell' remote places.

5. Designers view a model in a passive stereographic projection through polarized 3D goggles.

Alvise Simondetti brings a unique perspective to prototyping through his role as associate within Arup's 'Foresight' team, where his work ranges in scope from the broad (the behaviours of large numbers of people in such complex spaces as transport interchanges) to the narrow (evaluating the listening experience from every seat in a concert hall). Prototyping for Simondetti is perhaps a more esoteric activity than it is for many designers. Certainly, he views it as being more than merely practical, defining the prototype as something between 'primal', in the sense of being the original, and 'progenitor', in the Latin sense of the parent of the resulting species. Such a definition blurs the boundaries between the model and the prototype. Simondetti finds that, as end users have such diverse views of what a model is, it is perhaps better to use the word 'prototyping' instead, especially with 'non-specialist' clients when all they are being shown is, in fact, a 3D model.

For the prototype to be effective in communicating the proposed design to a less specialist audience, it is important for it to be made at full scale. For the specialist, by contrast, the prototype can be relatively abstract and produced at any scale.

How, then, to present a large and complex project intended, for example, to offer the non-specialist the chance to interact with the proposed wayfinding at a transport terminal, which obviously cannot be prototyped at full scale? Full virtual reality (VR) has become an unexpectedly useful adjunct to the client conversation in this regard,

4–5

6–7

8–9

6. Digital environments for experiential design, enhancing designers' perception, 2010–12: Exploring the new western concourse at King's Cross station in London through a computer-assisted virtual environment (CAVE) at the University of Reading, UK.

7. A digital, 3D representation of acoustic performance. In this example, the acoustic source is a string trio, with each instrument represented by a differently coloured isosurface. The size of each isosurface represents loudness, while the bulges illustrate the direction of the sound. In the animated representation, the isosurfaces move as the trio plays a piece of music.

8. Designers in Arup's SoundLab, London, listen to a piece of music as it would be heard in various concert halls.

9. SoundLab's iPad interface allows designers to switch between different music and venues, whether existing or proposed.

with Arup being among the vanguard of immersive 3D stereoscopic environments used to assist decision-making in the design process.

This aspect of Arup's practice blurs even more definitional boundaries, calling into question whether 3D stereoscopic simulation is better described as 'experiential design'. Such a definition allows the public to engage with design decision-making in new ways, especially younger people already adept at playing video games. In Simondetti's opinion, effective stereoscopic 3D makes physical prototyping, modelling and mock-ups rather redundant in situations where it is the user's experience (behaviour) that is being explored. Digital mock-ups, therefore, have no special place in Simondetti's lexicon; to him, VR has the potential to lead architectural practice towards 'zero prototyping'. Taking lessons from the aeronautical industry, Simondetti points out that the first Boeing 787 Dreamliner flew without ever being physically prototyped.

Ultimately, in the sense that Simondetti uses the term, prototyping tests strategies. This can be done through a very rich and varied set of trials. Simondetti describes the pleasure of seeing a typical commuter attempt to find their way through a proposed redesign of Hong Kong's Admiralty Station, used by 15 per cent of the city's population every day. In almost the same breath, he discusses the singular story of a composer who used the Arup 3D stereoscopic environment to compose their music, experiencing it 'live' – as they proceeded – within a virtual representation of the future listeners' experience.

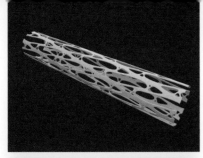

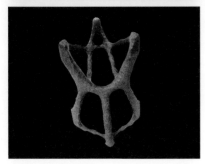

1–3

BKK Architects [Tim Black]

A means of interrogating the first formative idea

For Tim Black, director of Melbourne-based BKK Architects, a prototype in architecture is a means of interrogating an idea. A model explains the idea to others, while the prototype is a way for the designer to question their own proposals. Sometimes, the model and the modelling process itself have to be prototyped: not everything can be printed in 3D.

In manual physical-assembly processes, there is a serendipity that the digital realm can sometimes lack. However, in computational modelling, no two individuals will structure the model of a particular design problem exactly alike: individuals building a digital model of the same design problem will arrive at very different structures for the models. The trace of the individual, human approach and interrogation of the idea is always in the digital model too. Working with the Innovative Structures Group at RMIT University in Melbourne, BKK generated elegant organic structures for a series of footbridge proposals using evolutionary structural optimization. While the results appear naturalistic, the process and description of the form are highly computational and lend themselves to prototyping using such file-to-fabrication techniques as 3D printing.

There is no question that the physical model reveals things that the digital variety does not. Nevertheless, the interplay between simple computer programs and quick and dirty physical outputs has not yet reached its optimum. There is room for a great deal more 'back and forth' between the two, even with the help of free 3D modellers or by adding paper cutting and folding using a laser cutter into the mix.

1–2. Footbridge, Bi-Directional Evolutionary Structural Optimization (BESO), Innovative Structures Group at RMIT and Felicetti (engineers), Melbourne, Australia, 2009.

3. 3D print of 'evolved' chair structure.

4–6

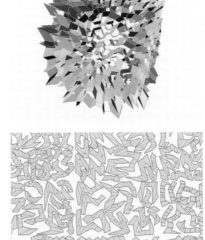

7–8

9–10

4–6. Suzhou Footbridge, Bi-Directional Evolutionary Structural Optimization (BESO), Innovative Structures Group at RMIT and Felicetti (engineers), Melbourne, Australia, 2013.

7–10. Design for *Pavilions of New Architecture*, Monash University Museum of Art (MUMA), Melbourne, Australia, 2005: Digital prototype of early concept model; cutting template for final model; a digital prototype; the completed design at MUMA.

Prototyping is not just about mocking up a space or designing an artefact. It is about testing an idea, whether that be an entire production and delivery system or a spatial design. Banks are rolling out scalable customer interfaces in ways that show that prototyping can be used to test business models in-depth and drive corporate entrepreneurialism. Start-ups are being led by designers who have seen an opportunity to create new ways of working for their customers.

It is important to make, touch and feel. In this sense the digital prototype is never quite enough. Clearly, we can create digital objects that are intriguing, exquisite, complex, rich and remarkable. However, if you are in the business of architecture, then you really have to ground the work in the process of making as well. Following an explosion in the creation of new and interesting forms, many architects have turned to the question of how one actually makes these things at the interface between digital design and digital fabrication. That said, the 'lab to fab' dream of total integration is still a way off.

Given the digital tools to which it has access, BKK produces a great deal of conceptual work. In the future, more architects may become programmers and embrace a more abstract mode of thought, but being able to use one's hands will remain critical. In the case of *Pavilions of New Architecture*, an exhibition of 1:3 prototype pavilions held at Monash University Museum of Art in Melbourne in 2005, BKK had no idea whether it could actually build its design, so physical prototyping was essential.

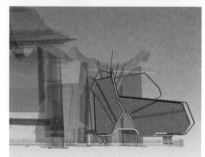

1–3

1–3. 55/02, Cock Stoor, Kielder Water
and Forest Park, Northumberland, UK,
2009: This project was a speculative
investigation into the difference between
digital modelling and physical installation.

3 · 83

← Techniques
2.2 / p. 27 / Mock-ups
2.4 / p. 37 / CNC Revolution
2.8 / p. 53 / Virtual Prototyping

Bob Sheil

Taking on an unknown as a challenge: an attempt to break new ground

Bob Sheil is as comfortable in the world of design experimentation as he is as head of a leading international school of architecture (the Bartlett, part of University College London). For Sheil, all buildings are prototypes. In particular, he sees the prototype as a way of breaking new ground in architecture, and not merely as a means of addressing a physical or technical issue. He stretches the term 'prototyping' to include testing the way buildings are used, the materials from which they are made, the way they are constructed and the way they are procured. The prototype, he believes, can also be used to explore the possibilities of file-to-factory construction. In his opinion, prototypes ask the questions but should not be expected to provide all the answers, regardless of whether the design insights sought are material, constructional or behavioural.

For Sheil, the distinction between models and prototypes has become more blurred than ever. A decade ago the model was seen as a purely representational tool, while the prototype was positioned to demonstrate actions and performance. The dominance of the digital in the realm between design and manufacturing has introduced fresh ambiguities, he believes, such that the role of the design model is no longer clear. Such ambiguities have led to a significant change in contemporary design practice, to the extent that the workshop now plays a more complementary role to that of the studio than ever before.

In design experimentation, the prototype is a means of examining and discussing the framing of the design question; prototypes, in other words,

9

7–8

4–6

4–6. 55/02: Pre-production design development, including an early prototype of structural shell in CNC-cut and CNC-folded plate steel.

7–9. Views of the assembled structure *in situ*.

can prototype the prototype. Sheil believes that the current practice of applying new tools to traditional modes of building procurement, with conventional client–planner–designer–user relationships, is limiting. If we invert our perception of the role of technology in architecture, seeing it as a way of releasing potential rather than an aid to maintaining the status quo, we might escape from the push to build the digitally rendered image. Evidence for this is the growing propensity among such schools as the Bartlett, the Architectural Association in London and the ICD in Stuttgart to design small, experimental pavilions as full-scale prototypes, thereby allowing the 'design and technology of production' equation to be investigated.

For the first time, building technology has properly entered the Bartlett campus, not as a way for students to find out how things are done, but as a means of allowing them to consider through prototyping how things might be done in the future. The difference between prototypes-as-experimental-design in practice and schools is the narrower focus in practice on performance aspects; in the schools, by contrast, experimentation through prototyping has the freedom to be significantly more ambitious. At the Bartlett, for instance, first-year students used to be kept away from the digital arena in order to ensure that the architectural sensibility of head-eye-hand was developed. Now, they learn an instinctive kind of sensibility around digital modes of representation and CNC-aided prototyping from the moment they set foot in the classroom.

1–3

1–3. INDEX: Award Pavilions, Copenhagen, 2011: The brief for this project was to design eight lightweight, transportable, carbon fibre-reinforced outdoor pavilions for the display of award-winning products and prototypes in a travelling exhibition. The challenge was to reduce the energy impact of the exhibition, which was scheduled to visit several international design fairs.

3 · 84

Greg Lynn

Whenever we try something new or unfamiliar, a prototype pops up

For Ohio-born designer Greg Lynn, architectural prototyping implies two very different things. The first is the rapid prototype, which he defines as a piece of geometry that, via a machine path, produces a physical object. The second is the prototype as a device for encouraging a builder or fabricator to do something differently. Having found that rapid prototyping rarely contributes to the design process, and despite being a pioneer of the technology, Lynn believes that it does not provoke any creative thinking about material, structure or assembly. In contrast, conventional prototyping generates a design feedback loop, changing the workflow as well as the relationship with fabricators and builders. Indeed, in terms of improving the dialogue with the project's eventual makers, he claims to get far more from conventional prototyping than is possible with the rapid variety.

For Lynn, modelling differs from prototyping by being more abstract in its intentions; prototyping, regardless of scale, anticipates both material selection and construction. Mock-ups, by contrast, are the implied, full-scale objects that are produced for approval further down the line. Lynn finds that the distinction between mock-ups and prototypes can be tantamount to splitting hairs, given that, on occasion, they are one and the same. One important difference is that the mock-up is often set up to verify the built object, while the prototype might be positioned to verify the concept.

Prototypes are integral to Lynn's practice, Greg Lynn Form (GLF). That said, Lynn believes that they do not have to test every aspect of a design. With the Blobwall (2005), for instance, the team looked at how

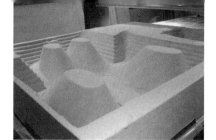

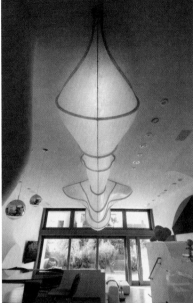

8–9

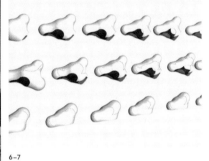

6–7

4–5

4–5. Bloom House, Southern California, 2010.

6–7. Blobwall, Los Angeles, CA, 2005: The Blobwall is composed of rotomolded hollow-plastic bricks that are custom-cut using a CNC robot arm, assembled and heat-welded into freestanding walls and enclosures.

8–9. Ravioli Chair, 2005: Designed for Vitra, the Ravioli Chair is now part of the permanent collection of both the Museum of Modern Art, New York, and the Art Institute of Chicago.

the individual components would interlock. In the case of the Bloom House (2010), by contrast, the qualities tested were merely translucency and the diffusion of light. The singularity of purpose is another defining principle that distinguishes the prototype from the mock-up.

Lynn is very positive about the existence of digital prototypes, but takes care to distinguish a rapid prototype – the pure digital expression of material as a model – from situations where printed components, such as flatware printed directly in metal or boat parts printed in fibre-reinforced nylon, come together as a prototype. He has no hesitation in making design decisions, where appropriate, from digital representations on a computer screen, but does not consider this prototyping. Only physical objects count as prototypes, albeit partially or fully digitally produced.

Inevitably, prototypes for Lynn are part of a drive towards the unknown, always leading to innovation. In more familiar circumstances, or when there is a level of abstraction involved, he regards the physical manifestation of a design in progress as a model; whenever the practice is pursuing something new or unfamiliar, a prototype pops up.

GLF does not necessarily absorb the costs of prototyping, as others might, perceiving that these should be built into the fabricators' bids. The practice, however, has far more prototyping equipment than most builders and fabricators, so Lynn concedes that it frequently bears the burden of prototyping. On the other hand, he often finds that contractors have made unsolicited experimental prototypes for their own purposes.

In this section, the featured examples highlight the dilemma of whether to view prototyping as a process or a product, or indeed both. When it comes to assessing the relative value of prototyping as an activity – an avenue of design enquiry – as opposed to a physical or virtual manifestation of that enquiry, there is potential for some ambivalence.

In several of the examples that follow, user experience is a key component of the design process. As such, not only does the design require development in such a way that the experience can be tested *en vivo*, but also the viability of the completed project has to be confirmed through subsequent testing. Crowd Productions, for instance, treats prototyping as a design-research strategy, seeking the gradual materialization of an idea while evolving and testing the parameters, many of which emerge only during the design process. By necessity, design has to embrace a certain amount of unpredictability.

Michael Hensel treats prototyping as a means of confronting the 'messiness of context'. In such cases, the creative disorder of the design studio is contrasted with orderly experimentation in the lab. For Hyperbody, treating prototyping as an amalgam of process and product lifts the designer from 'prototyping by pavilion' to prototyping interactive building design. This offers all the challenges that embracing new technologies in unusual contexts presents, with the added problem of trying to predict the viability of completely novel user experiences. Asif Khan is in similar territory, and the example from Foster + Partners highlights the different needs and priorities of diverse disciplines working together on the same project. Here, industrial designers, who are used to prototyping the entire design, have to compare notes with architects, who are more familiar with prototyping only part of a design, and often with a far greater degree of abstraction.

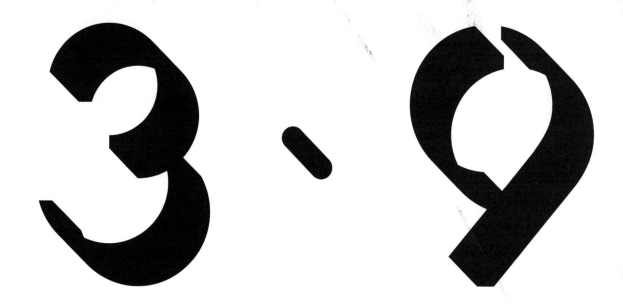

3.9

Process or Product

1–3

← Techniques
2.2 / p. 27 / Mock-ups
2.4 / p. 37 / CNC Revolution
2.7 / p. 49 / Enter the Robot

Foster + Partners

[Mike Holland / Xavier De Kestelier / James White]

99.9% there

At Foster + Partners there is a wide range of design expertise under one roof, including industrial and furniture design. For Mike Holland – partner and industrial designer – a prototype is a relatively refined, full-scale version of something, built when you are getting close to the final piece. The earlier, rough, diagrammatic models on the way to the prototype Holland describes as sketch models and mock-ups. These can start life as a torn, folded piece of paper or, as in the example of a business-class seat for an airline, a simple, full-scale foam-block mock-up for looking at the overall dimensions and angle of the seat but without any design applied to it. These mock-ups are expendable, and can be chopped into or reshaped. By contrast, a prototype for Holland is 99.9 per cent 'there' (unless, that is, it leads to substantial changes that could only come about as a result of seeing the prototype or, on occasion, the decision to start again).

In architecture, you cannot prototype the whole building, so you mock up parts of it or simulate its performance digitally; in industrial design, however, most objects are prototyped in their entirety. The industrial-design prototype needs to be very close to the final artefact. You should be able to touch, feel and understand the interfaces, as well as test the structure and materiality, so it is always physical. And with the increasing ability to make physical versions quickly, more things are tested in the physical realm.

Foster + Partners' Molteni Teso Table (2013) is based on the deceptively simple idea of cutting slits in a circular disc and pressing it into a 3D form. As the filigree structure opens up from two dimensions into three, the intermediate struts twist and the material stretches. That

1–3. Molteni Teso Table, Milan, Italy, 2013: The table's base is formed by a robotic arm, which presses and twists a perforated disc of steel into a tough, tapered cylinder.

4 (opposite). A view of the table's geometry.

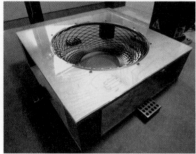

5–6

7–8

9

5. Molteni Teso Table: Prior to being formed by the robot arm, a scaled-down, laser-cut steel disc is clamped at its rim between an acrylic sheet and a plywood box.

6. The disc after being pressed. This process allowed the designers to study the deformation effect and make adjustments to the cut pattern in order to achieve the desired structural form.

7. A full-size prototype of the table is inspected at Molteni's factory in Milan.

8. These tables were used to explore different surface treatments and finishes, including anodizing, electroplating, physical vapour deposition (PVD) and powder-coating.

9. A final prototype with glass tabletop in place.

10–11. 1:1 laser-cut card sections used to study and compare various cut patterns.

deformation gives the table its rigidity and strength. Of the twenty or thirty prototypes made using different materials and different cutting patterns, some failed from the start; with others, the longer the struts, the more they twisted and the stronger they became. The physical modelling was playful, with trial and error and a willingness to make mistakes proving to be by far the most efficient ways of testing the various options. Exploiting the speed of digital remodelling via laser and water-jet cutting, the designers worked first at scale and then 1:1, with paper and eventually metal. The use of a physics engine to emulate the table's behaviour digitally would have been a poor alternative.

The table, like most of the practice's other furniture commissions, was developed in partnership with the manufacturer, which had taken over the making by the pre-production prototyping stage. The table, however, was *designed* by making. Over the last ten or fifteen years, CNC technology has transformed the design process, including prototyping. It is much more economical to print, cut or mill numerous models, even at full scale, than it was to hand-construct one full-scale model using a foam scrapper with a rasp, even though there was design evolution in the making of such a singular model over a period of two or three weeks. In the age of plug-and-play 3D printing, the keys to success are choosing the right tool for the job and remaining in touch with material properties and behaviour. The Teso Table prototypes were used to test aesthetics, the strength of the structure, its interface with the tabletop, and the production process.

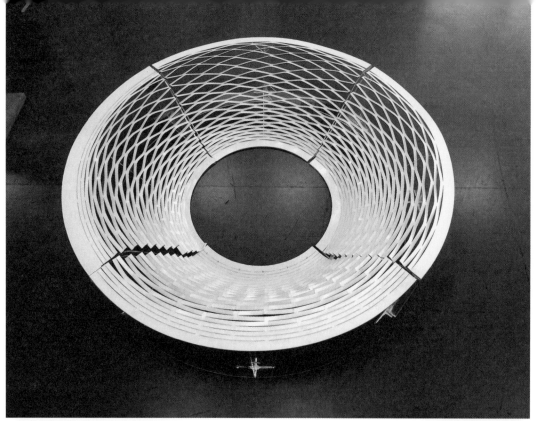

1–2

3 · 92

Asif Khan

Everything is a prototype for the next thing

1. Beatbox Pavilion, London 2012 Summer Olympics: The 1:200 competition model of the pavilion.

2. A 1:25 sectional model of the pavilion, illustrating the colour and arrangement of the ETFE cushions for client approval.

3–5. 1:1 construction mock-up used to determine the optimal installation of the ETFE cushions both to the substructure and between adjacent frames.

6–9. A 1:1 ETFE cushion prototype undergoes testing at iart's workshop in Basel, Switzerland. The prototype enabled the electrical, mechatronic and sound engineers, as well as the programmers, to test the elements for which they were responsible in conjunction with the work of other teams. This 'agile' process of direct feedback allowed for the rapid development of the finished cushion.

Despite having graduated from the Bartlett only in 2004, London-born architect Asif Khan has achieved an international reputation and profile for a series of spectacular, forward-looking projects. Two recent projects alone attest to his desire to push the design, innovation and technology envelope. Built for the London 2012 Summer Olympics, the Beatbox Pavilion (a collaboration with Swedish architect Pernilla Ohrstedt for Coca-Cola) featured 200 touch-sensitive ETFE cushions, which could be 'played' by visitors as they climbed up the pavilion's ramp. The resulting sounds, which ranged from athletes' heartbeats to an arrow hitting a target, were complemented by an interactive light installation inside the structure. The MegaFaces pavilion, conceived for the 2014 Winter Olympics in Sochi, is another building that seeks to both communicate with its users and provide a spectacle for onlookers. Composed of 11,000 actuators, each equipped with full-colour LEDs, the 60-metre-long kinetic façade of the pavilion is able to recreate in high relief the faces of visitors to the building.

Given the technical challenges, scale of ambition and sheer audacity of Khan's projects, the viewer is forced to ponder the design pathway involved in realizing such innovation. What role does the prototype play in such work, which stretches across a far wider range of disciplines than a typical architectural project? And compared to a more traditional building, is prototyping such interactive architecture a profoundly different activity?

Khan is careful not to draw on any bombastic definitions, seeing the prototype as incorporating aspects of functional behaviour that will be

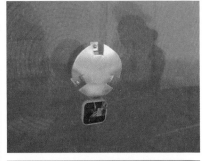

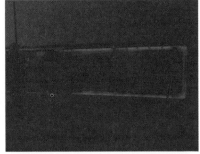

3–5

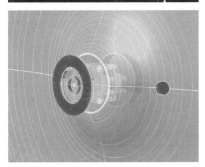

10–11. Beatbox Pavilion: ETFE cushions
in production at Taiyo's workshop in
Sauerlach, Germany. The cushions used an
aluminium frame designed by the architects
to meet stiffness criteria set out by the
structural engineers and to accommodate
electrical, audio and data routes identified
by the systems engineers within an elegant
proportion. Each performative characteristic
of the cushion was identified through earlier
physical and digital prototypes made by
the relevant team member.

12. A 3D model of the high-frequency
'exciter' speaker assembly attached
to the ETFE membrane.

13. The final prototype ETFE cushion
installed in the Beatbox Pavilion. The
pavilion was opened to the public early so
the cushions could be field-tested, both for
responsiveness and for robustness. Note
the capacitive sensor antenna silkscreened
to the surface of the cushion.

10–13

6–9

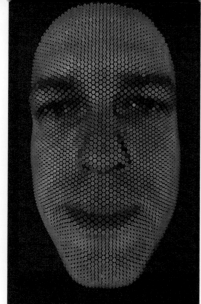

14–15

16–17

18–19

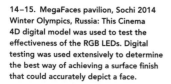

14–15. MegaFaces pavilion, Sochi 2014 Winter Olympics, Russia: This Cinema 4D digital model was used to test the effectiveness of the RGB LEDs. Digital testing was used extensively to determine the best way of achieving a surface finish that could accurately depict a face.

16–17. 1:1 mock-up of the 3D scanning booth, with head-positioning rig for testing the scanning process.

18. The elastomeric fabric used on the pavilion undergoes testing. The aim of the test was to understand the force required to deform the material to the optimum distance from a level plane.

19. Test version of the motor used to drive the actuators. The size of the motor and its casing determined the number of acuators used on the pavilion.

central to the final building. While a prototype for Khan will most likely be the same scale as the object it symbolically represents, the symbolism itself absolves it from taking on the role of a mock-up depicting the look of the project; nor does it need to take on the role of the model as a scaled representation of the ideas at play. The particularity of the prototype and its meaning within interactive work are important to Khan's practice, because the name given to the item placed on the table for discussion – model, mock-up or prototype – can make all the difference to the conversation, either opening it up or closing it down, depending on the overall objective of the meeting and the context.

Digital prototyping also has a role to play in Khan's practice. Interactivity is a computed, near real-time outcome, and requires computed simulation. The digital prototype can therefore be the ultimate hybrid of analogue material confection and digital back end – just as an engineer testing a car engine does not necessarily need to know nor represent what the car body will look like at certain times during the design process. Ultimately, a prototype for Khan does not need to lead to an artefact – digital, analogue or both – nor, necessarily, to look like the final outcome. Rather, it needs to embody processes that are at least analogous to those that will be used for the finished structure. Moreover, each prototype might be an essential step along a journey calling on a series of prototypes leading to the next thing … 'a kind of notch in the bed post', as Khan himself puts it.

20–22

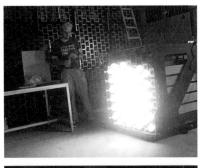

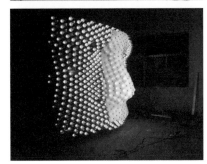

23–26

20. MegaFaces pavilion: Testing the RGB LEDs within a translucent, 3D-printed sphere.

21. A prototype of an actuator tip, consisting of a translucent, moulded-polypropylene sphere and a rod with a magnetic end cap for attaching the elastomeric fabric.

22. Component array to determine the optimum arrangement of the actuator tips. They were eventually arranged in a diagrid pattern, which achieved the smoothest replication of facial features.

23. Working actuator prototypes mounted in a steel-framed module housing.

24. Actuators being tested at full extension.

25. The 'thousand pin test': final testing of a sample number of actuators prior to shipping to Sochi.

26. A group of actuators is lit and extended to form the eyes, nose and upper lip of a scanned face.

27–29. The completed MegaFaces pavilion in operation.

27–29

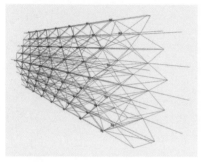

1–3

3 · 93

← Techniques
2.3 / p. 31 / Prototyping Performance
2.4 / p. 37 / CNC Revolution
2.7 / p. 49 / Enter the Robot

ONL [Oosterhuis_Lénárd]

Prototypes are 1:1 interactive pathways to the end product

Kas Oosterhuis and colleagues at Dutch architectural practice ONL [Oosterhuis_Lénárd] have a singular vision: the creation of customized environments tuned to the individual needs of the client with the capability of being responsive to ever-changing internal and external environments, different users and different uses. At ONL, information communication technology (ICT) is key to every part of the design process – from conception to completed project. Just as procurement paths need to change radically, Oosterhuis contends that architectural practice needs to evolve rapidly too, in order to take advantage of new technologies.

Beyond bold and progressive prognostications, ONL puts its convictions into practice. Early projects – such the Salt Water Pavilion at Neeltje Jans (1997), a collaboration with Lars Spuybroek of NOX Architects – demonstrated a fascination with interactivity, at least within an interior environment. By 2003 the practice was experimenting with wholly interactive built forms, one of most radical being Muscle NSA, a giant, blue, inflatable rubber 'bladder' created for the *Non-standard Architecture* exhibition at the Centre Pompidou (2003). Muscle NSA presented visitors to the exhibition with an architectural space that could change its shape in response to inputs from the various sensors that surrounded it. A network of pneumatic 'muscles', which could expand and contract in reaction to the sensor data, enabled the structure to reconfigure itself. Being inside the space as it changed in response to otherwise invisible exterior activity was a distinctly unnerving experience.

1–3. Soundbarrier, A2 motorway, Utrecht, Netherlands, 2006: Inside the point-cloud model; a wireframe model; the northern end of the barrier.

4–5

6–7

8–9

4–9. Soundbarrier: 1:1 mock-up
and panel testing.

10

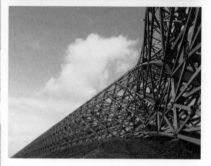

13–14

11–12

10–14. Soundbarrier: Views
of the completed sound barrier.

While developing experimental interactive prototypes with students in the guise of Hyperbody – Ooterhuis's research laboratory established at TU Delft in 2000 – ONL has focused on experimenting more deeply with its non-standard and interactive architecture. Oosterhuis regards the working prototype as having two defining characteristics. The first is that it is active, in the sense that a project's interactive 'action' has to be physically tested, not simulated. This philosophy was first put into practice in the Muscle NSA project and continues today. The second is that it is 1:1.

Characteristically for Oosterhuis, the prototype is necessarily the pathway to the final product, and never the final product itself, which he regards as a mock-up. For the sort of work that drives the practice, models are seen as representations. They are also regarded as not being especially informative, particularly as models of interactive architecture tend to provide little in the way of useful information. Digital prototypes have a role at the practice, but in the sense of a 'game'. Within the design process at ONL, the digital prototype features as a 'quick and dirty' component with its own targets. That is, it has to 'work', just as the 1:1 working prototype has to perform.

In the experience of the practice, while old habits die hard in terms of the perceived obligations of contractors to engage in prototyping as part of the designer–builder dialogue (i.e. they are disinclined to participate unless paid specifically to do so), changes are afoot. A new generation of prototyping tools is emerging, including 3D printers, CNC plasma

15–16

17–18

19–20

cutters, and so on. Such developments are seen by Oosterhuis as signs of progress, although he acknowledges that there is still some way to go.

Clearly, prototypes are being used within ONL to test behaviours. Moreover, they are being used in a series of defined iterations, with each one formulated as a quantum leap from its predecessor: Oosterhuis and colleagues are not fans of advancing a project through endless tweaking. No distinction is made between industrial and architectural prototypes in this regard, as the practice looks at the design of buildings from a far wider range of angles than is usual.

ONL is as quizzical about the narrowness of traditional architectural practice as it is about pavilions that are built to test, say, construction techniques: neither, it believes, is prototyping on a grand scale. Oosterhuis feels that it is only by stepping beyond the particularities of the experimental pavilions that are popping up globally (seen by many as radical experimentation) to prototyping interactive building design that society will see a meaningful advance in architecture framed on the technological possibilities of our age.

15. iWeb, Delft University, Netherlands, 2002–14: An aerial view of the iWeb's non-standard steel structure.

16–18. Exterior views of the completed building.

19. The interior of the iWeb was lit with LEDs.

20. Spraying on the interior insulation.

1–3

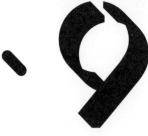

3 · 94

← Techniques
2.2 / p. 27 / Mock-ups
2.8 / p. 53 / Virtual Prototyping

Crowd Productions [Michael Trudgeon]

A hearth for a conversation

For Michael Trudgeon, design director at Melbourne-based Crowd Productions, prototyping has three axes. The first relates to what extent the prototype looks and feels like the final product; the second to how inclusive it is, meaning the degree to which you want to use it in the conversation with the client and other parties; and the third to functionality. All three are controlled by cost and time, and valued in terms of the feedback they provide.

Excluding users from the conversation about innovation seemed foolish to Crowd Productions, a design studio focused on customer and staff experiences, so it has thought long and hard about how to develop prototypes that are not mere proofs of concept, but which include all sorts of functionality. In this way, the prototype becomes a kind of hearth around which to converse. The modernist idea of change fascinates the designers at Crowd, but change challenges existing assumptions; it is uncomfortable and risky. By allowing all the stakeholders to experience what is being proposed, and then inviting them to bring their knowledge and experience to the conversation, risk is managed through collective intelligence. The prototype thus becomes a catalyst to conversation.

It is important for large commercial clients to understand the monetary value of design, beginning with interactive prototyping. In many instances, such prototyping serves to optimize the money-making aspects of a business, especially customer services in organizations with multiple outlets, such as banks and cinemas. Where there is a series of

1. Spatial and strategic prototyping programme for CUA, Brisbane, Australia, 2012–14: Consisting of a large number of cardboard boxes, the prototype space was continuously 'redesigned' in response to user feedback and the emergence of new ideas.

2–3. The space was used in part to test new banking procedures, with management, staff and customers all participating. The process was fully documented for the purposes of assessing outcomes and mapping user journeys.

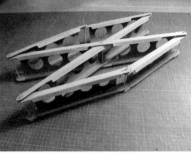

6–7

8

4–5

4. Digital cinema capsule for ACMI (Australian Centre for the Moving Image), Melbourne, Australia, 2002–05: A meeting at the workshop of Riva Fab, the principal fabricators, to discuss the design-detailing process over pizza and beer.

5. The development of a multi-user 'telescopic' system for the control screen. The specific functional geometry was refined using scaled-timber prototypes.

6. A cardboard model of the final scissor-arm support system, optimized for weight.

7. A full-scale stainless-steel prototype of the support system, created to test its performance.

8. The completed digital cinema capsule showing elements of the partition system and the fibre-optically lit rear 'blister pack' portrait wall.

commissions, the feedback from the initial design helps to improve any subsequent work.

Prototyping is a core activity at Crowd, and all kinds of models may be involved. A prototype might include a suite of things, from a room-sized space mocked up quickly and cheaply from laser-cut wood and fabric to a beautiful scale model, sprayed and mounted at chin height. In each case the intention is to engage the imagination in as many ways as possible, to stimulate exchange. The digital has a place in this, from 3D fly-throughs to more immersive technology, such as the Oculus Rift, a head-mounted virtual-reality (VR) display. The aim is to make this kind of experience as accessible as possible, which on some occasions might mean switching from Oculus Rift to Dive (a device for turning a smartphone into a VR headset), free smartphone apps or simple 3D glasses. In the short term at least, digital prototyping will not displace all physical experiences: materiality, smell, air movement and temperature can be vital in communicating some design ideas.

The focus on digital technology has drawn many people away from physical engagement – the ability, for example, to pull things apart in the garage and remake them. Finding ways to fuse the digital with the physical is of critical importance. Trudgeon believes that people with particular analogue, or making, skills can generally use digital tools in a more powerful way. Similarly, to get the best from prototyping, Crowd uses 'bodystorming', the physically immersive version of brainstorming.

1–3

3·95

OCEAN Design Research Association

Complexity of context

Michael Hensel, founding member of OCEAN, likes prototypes that confront the messiness of context, as opposed to those that have been developed in laboratory conditions. He has been working with prototypes since 2000, and does not know how his group would be able to do its design-research work without them. In the context of design as research, he also likes the term 'functional model' – a model that is not purely about form and aesthetics, but which also demonstrates how something works. Depending on scale, the functional model can overlap with the prototype. Generally speaking, physical forces do not scale well, so where the design-research question is about such forces, at least a partial full-scale prototype is needed at some point in the design process.

While simulating context is extremely complicated, Hensel believes that real-world context can be very revealing, throwing up all sorts of surprises. He cites the example of a series of small membrane canopies at the Oslo School of Architecture and Design that unexpectedly encountered two of the most extreme Norwegian winters in forty years, one after the other. The snow accumulated on the canopies and, after reaching a certain depth, started to close all the gaps between the membranes, creating a huge and extremely heavy frozen 'sail' with all sorts of unanticipated horizontal loading.

In the case of a new community centre for the town of Pumanque in Chile (2014), some of the planks that make up the wooden decks were removed by vandals and used for firewood – an unanticipated cultural

1–3. Nested Catenaries Phase 2, Oslo, Norway, 2011: Partial prototype under construction.

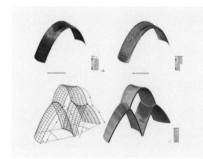

4–5

6–9

10–13

4–5. Structural simulation and analysis for the Nested Catenaries project.

6–9. Nested Catenaries Phase 1, Oslo, Norway, 2010: Brick construction experiments.

10–13. Nested Catenaries Phase 2, Open City Ritoque, Chile, 2012: Pilot project in context.

14–15

16–17

18–19

14–19. Community centre, Pumanque, Chile, 2014: Pilot project in context.

contingency that would have required very particular approaches to materials and fixings. Another example of unexpected feedback from prototyping in Chile concerns the longevity of stainless-steel cable. Calculations were made based on the site's proximity to the Pacific Ocean and its salt-laden air. But no one anticipated the effect of a nearby copper refinery, which added atmospheric acidity that, in combination with the salty air, corroded the cable within just one year.

Typically, the team at OCEAN tries to build 1:1 prototypes of the most complicated parts of a design so that they know how to realize them once they are on site. For the kind of academic research and student projects conducted by OCEAN – projects often built in as little as seven days – there are often enormous logistical challenges. In the case of a project in Patagonia, for instance, the site could only be reached by a small boat, which had to carry not only the project team but also all the tools and materials except the timber, thereby providing a rigorous exercise in logistics and planning. Hensel notes that it is good for architecture students to enter the world of the builder. In the case of the Flying Compression canopy (2013), a tensegrity project in Nusfjord in the Lofoten district of Norway, the team had to build in freezing conditions and gale-force winds, using seawater to clear snow from the site.

Architectural practice is another potentially messy context for university research centres. But collaboration with practice is vital if basic research-through-design, as well as early risk-taking, to find its way into the built environment beyond small prototypical interventions.

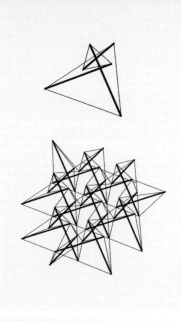

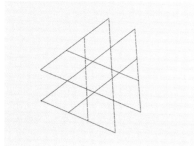

20–21. Flying Compression canopy,
Nusfjord, Lofoten, Norway, 2013.

22–23. Together with a selection
of landscaped furniture, the Flying
Compression canopy provides an
outdoor eating area for a restaurant
on Nusfjord's harbour.

3.95 / OCEAN Design Research Association

Conclusion

In preparing this overview of the role of prototyping for the contemporary architect, we have drawn from in-depth conversations with a wide range of architects, designers and engineers seeking to establish some key fundamentals. We have been motivated to delve deeply into, and report on, the experimental aspects of their design practice by a desire to inspire, consolidating the field into a series of linked commonalities and identifying new knowledge emerging from architectural prototyping at a time when extraordinary digital techniques have become available. The organization of Part 3 is not intended to be strictly taxonomic, but rather to serve as a reference point in what is a rapidly widening field of constantly evolving possibility and opportunity. In considering prototyping in architecture today, how different is a compilation such as this one from an equivalent collection of insights from an architectural epoch other than our own, post-digital one?

Let us suspend the space-time continuum, then, and imagine a dinner party attended by some of the most influential creative thinkers from across the Renaissance and the centuries immediately following it, including Filippo Brunelleschi, Leonardo da Vinci, Michelangelo, Gian Lorenzo Bernini, Christopher Wren and Robert Hooke. As innovators of their day, they might well compare notes on their collective role in bringing architectural design and its related scientific and technical discourses out from the masons' yards and into their studios. Representational spatial abstractions as models, along with sketches, templates and other 2D drawings, would be common to all these architects – as much the means to extemporize their designs as to explain the building tasks across a newly created distinction between the designers and those charged with realizing their projects. Were the steps to Michelangelo's Laurentian Library in Florence (1571) or Bernini's arrangement of natural lighting for his *Ecstasy of Saint Teresa* (1647–52) their own prototypes, or did they have other, *a priori* means to determine the success of their concepts in development? Was there much difference in the way Brunelleschi, Michelangelo and Christopher Wren worked out the structures for their respective domes, and, if there was, how would they describe and compare their techniques at the dinner table?

A combination of descriptive geometry, applied scientific knowledge and technical ingenuity would tie them together as designers in the same way as it distinguishes them, as a group, from the Gothic masters who preceded them. One can imagine our time-travelling diners referring to their medieval forebears as pattern-makers and pattern-followers, and reading their own great achievements in comparison as an ongoing series of refinements. By contrast, they would probably regard their own master works collectively as an ongoing sequence of visionary projects-as-prototypes advancing towards a future that they were consciously creating to be different from the present. No doubt they would also see their apprentices as having a different role from that of the medieval masons, with the participation of students in their studio-based experimentation perceived as being an essential part of the education of future architects, compared to the more prosaic skill acquisition within the medieval mason's yard.

With the advent of the Industrial Revolution, new materials and new techniques saw further specialization, with the Renaissance-born architect-engineers beginning to bifurcate into separate professions (to different degrees, depending on national predilection). With the emergence of the great technical universities, architects became professionals further distanced not only from the sites of construction but also from the laboratories of scientific and technical investigation that had coloured the practice of earlier generations of pre-professional building designers. If we suspend our space-time continuum still further, and invite to the dinner party such masters of the Modern Movement as Alvar Aalto, Le Corbusier, Mies van der Rohe and Louis Kahn, how well would these newcomers relate to their colleagues from an earlier age? They would be respectful, of course, but would they regard their prototyping methods and design goals to be from the same stable, or a significant advancement on those of their seniors?

History would give them an awareness of the contributions of their Renaissance and, later, their Enlightenment peers, but perhaps they would be inclined to boast of progress and the post-industrial technical achievements from which they had all been able to profit. From their points of view, the Renaissance masters would surely be incredulous of the unimaginable performance opportunities yielded by steel and concrete. Perhaps, however, they would also be incredulous of the relative poverty of expression in much of the Modernist portfolio, given the opportunities offered by new materials and scientific advances, particularly if the conversation turned to the nature of studio-based architectural research. With notable exceptions within their individual portfolios, as well as within those of such relative outliers as Buckminster Fuller, Jean Prouvé, Frei Otto and others, the Modernist approach would be seen by the elders as predominantly a methodology, with prototyping notably an exception within the twentieth-century studio repertoire compared with today, still less in the education of future architects. While space and light, geometry and form were drivers for the designers of the pre-industrialized age, would they find the post-industrial love of the straight line, the right angle, the vertical, the manifesto and the role of the section as a principal design 'device' as compelling as their own predilection for experimentation and prototyping shifts within a constantly evolving paradigm?

Oversimplification this may well be, but even if not universally appraised as a deliberate and contrived reductionism, the Modern Movement certainly brought a uniformity and conformity to post-Second World War architectural education worldwide. In many places, experimentation through prototyping was not central to architects' education, which is what makes institutions such as the Architectural Association School of Architecture in London and Cranbrook Academy of Art in Bloomfield Hills, Michigan, so exceptional. It is also what has led to architects from these institutions, plus others who received at least a partial art education, developing a different set of sensibilities. Let us imagine extending our dinner party to include anyone from the wide range of protagonists featured in this book, such as Eva Jiricna, Greg Lynn, Kerstin Thompson, Chris Sharples, Jeanne Gang and Enric Ruiz-Geli. How would the design approaches of today's leading designers appear when contrasted with those of earlier periods?

The extended dinner-party guest list now features key representatives from, first, the pre-industrial, pre-professional epoch; secondly, the post-industrial, professional technocracy epoch; and thirdly, the post-digital and, most likely, a more significantly post-professional epoch. Taking an idea through to design development and on to a constructed architectural wonder would obviously be the principal objective held in common across the historical divide, but significant differences in design approaches would also be apparent. Curiously, the post-digital proponents could well have more in common with their Renaissance peers than the others, especially with regard to experimentation and rule-shifting. It is hard to imagine that the older participants at this hypothetical symposium would not be absolutely fascinated by the extraordinary range of opportunities available to the current generation of designers in charge of creating the built environment. As the projects in this volume attest, opportunities provided by the likes of rapid prototyping, robots, machines that print materials and machines that carve and shape materials have become financially affordable and practically available, even with desktop potential. Consequently, they have been brought into the studio as creative complements to sketch pad and pencil. The Internet has facilitated accessibility to data and know-how for the instant application of new knowledge to project development in real time. For many, virtual prototyping is a speedy and cost-effective adjunct to the physical prototype; in some rarer cases, it is regarded as a suitable proxy even for hands-on commitment.

Prototyping today is a key term in the contemporary designer's creative lexicon. As this book demonstrates, aspects of twenty-first-century prototyping would be completely unfamiliar to earlier generations of building designers, were they to be confronted by the actuality of the present. At the same time, the instinct and drive for experimentation within design is as manifest today as it has been since those motivated architects of the Renaissance pushed at the boundaries by treating each new project as the next opportunity for prototyping the great architecture that propels each generation forward.

Directory

Glossary

analogue

Most often used to describe a signal that is continuous and potentially variable, as opposed to a digital signal, which is expressed in binary form as a series of 0s (for 'off') and 1s (for 'on'). In design, *analogue* has come to be associated with traditional, hand-based manufacturing processes, with *digital* referring to the use of a computer to carry out the same processes.

CAD

The commonly used acronym for computer-aided design. Using appropriate software, a computer can be used to undertake tasks previously ascribed to such *analogue* media as pen and paper.

cellular automaton

Drawn from computer science and mathematics, a cellular automaton is a single cell located within a grid of cells that is finite but can be any given number. Each cell is centred within a neighbourhood of cells, and is imbued with a finite set of states, such as 'on' and 'off'. The operational states of an individual cell can be ordered with respect to its neighbours through a set of rules, thereby becoming the inputs to *computer scripts* for the purposes of discovery. In science, cellular automata might be used to research the growth patterns of given organisms, for example, whereas in design they can be used to generate potentially useful outcomes from a given set of cells working with a defined set of initial states and rules.

computer scripting

In the context of *CAD*, many programs can be customized by the user through the writing of additional computer code. This process, referred to as 'scripting' (or 'coding'), enables the user to increase the pace of their design experimentation and boost their productivity.

defined behaviour

In computation, *defined behaviour* refers to the coder/programmer being required to specify one particular feature for an implementation operation from a set of choices. In design computation, the designer is expressing their intention through exercising a choice, rather than letting it be the result of random selection.

digital

In computing, *digital* refers to the expression of information in binary form (i.e. as a series of 0s and 1s). In design, *digital* is often contrasted with *analogue*. 'Digital media', for instance, refers to the use of a computer to describe or represent an idea or design using suitable software, such as *CAD* programs for 2D drawing or 3D modelling. By contrast, *analogue* refers to traditional media being used for the same purpose, such as pen and paper for 2D drawing, and cardboard and glue in place of 3D printing.

electrophoresis

A laboratory technique used to separate molecules from one other based on size.

embedded implicit knowledge

Generated through social and/or professional interaction, implicit knowledge is knowledge that is tacitly understood within the group to which it is relevant, and which has not been made explicit. In *CAD*, the challenge is to codify implicit knowledge such that any related computation can be informed in a way that is sympathetic to the way the group works outside the computation environment; with *embedded implicit knowledge*, the opportunities for the computer to operate randomly are reduced.

Evolutionary Structural Optimization

Proposed by professors Mike Xie and Grant Steven in the 1990s, *Evolutionary Structural Optimization* (ESO) is based on the simple concept of strategically removing potentially redundant material and testing the viability of the resulting structural arrangement through iterative calculation. The eventual outcome is confirmed when the residual material has evolved towards being the optimum solution using the least amount of material.

explicit systems logic

In design computation, *explicit systems logic* is the 'explicit' representation of material behaviour. This enables a design to evolve through the use of *CAD* while taking into account real performance constraints, such as the extent to which a wooden slat can be twisted before it splits.

filament

3D printers are able to produce solid objects from a wide range of materials, such as powders that are fused together or solids that are melted and then extruded. Plastics, for example, are melted by the 3D printer and squirted as fine threads or filaments from a nozzle, like toothpaste from a tube. The filaments, which harden as they are precisely positioned, can be seen as fine layers in the resulting object.

moment of inertia

The geometrical and mechanical property used by engineers to calculate the deflection of a beam, for example, under loading. The stresses exerted on the material as it is externally loaded, as well as under its own weight, are components of the calculated moments of inertia.

multi-criteria optimization

Optimization is the process of determining the best set of parameters for arriving at an appropriate outcome. An example of optimization through design computation would be seeking the dimensions of a window as a single criterion in order to provide a defined amount of light to a room in a specified location. *Multi-criteria optimization* refers to a situation in which more than one outcome is sought in a given scenario; in the window example referred to, such outcomes might include not only providing a minimum amount of light but also ensuring that the window is sized appropriately so as not to produce too much heat gain.

multiple performance criteria

Used in a situation where, in seeking a desired outcome, a design has to meet more than one performance criteria, some of which may be in competition with each other. Indeed, in the world of design, realizing a particular outcome seldom involves satisfying just one such criteria. See also *multi-criteria optimization*.

particle systems

In design computation, *particle systems* are used to determine the likely response of a large number of objects to a defined event. Each particle in the system is an agent in the sense that it has properties and behaviours ascribed to it. Particle systems can be used to model a crowd's response to a particular environment, such as the likely behaviour of a large group of theatregoers leaving at the end of a show. Depending on the results of the model, the designer can ensure that sufficient doors with appropriate width are provided to ensure orderly egress.

rendering

The addition of colour, texture, light and shade to a 3D computer model of a building or object. Rendering can be relatively simple, revealing the basic form of what is being represented, or it can be highly realistic, to the extent that the rendered artefact becomes indistinguishable from the real thing (were it actually to exist).

system rules

Systems are complex arrangements of logical processes through which appropriate inputs can lead to desired outputs. Typically, systems do not operate randomly, but instead rely on a set of rules or protocols. These in turn are designed to provide answers to questions, solutions to problems and, in some cases, designed responses to clearly stated needs.

tensegrity

First used by Buckminster Fuller in the 1960s, *tensegrity* – a conflation of 'tensional integrity' – is the distinguishing property of a structure in which the elements of compression and tension accommodate forces in opposition, such that no two compression elements physically touch each other within a spatial system defined by a network of tensile cables or chains.

Index

Index

270

Practice Directory

Picture Credits

Acknowledgments

It is possible that, had we fully known what would be required, we might have hesitated to assemble the rich array of material that makes up this book. The unanticipated challenge arose from a slightly naive assumption on our part: that it would cost the fifty practices we approached for contributions little in the way of effort to look more closely at the engine behind their operation – the design process, rather than just the design outcome – and with it delve more deeply into their resources, beyond the readily accessible archives of pristine 'money shots' of completed projects. But we were asking them to take time out of their busy schedules to have an extended conversation with us, and then trawl through the less glamorous stuff of architectural endeavour in search of material that, in comparison to images of the finished buildings, would look scruffy and unfinished. More crucially, however, it would be highly revealing of the way in which they work with colleagues to refine their nascent designs and produce award-winning results from the crucible of experimentation – a process best described as prototyping for architecture.

In hindsight, could we have looked at, say, eight exemplars and dug more deeply within that reduced sample set? That might have been our initial intention, but as the project got underway we soon realized that such a limited sample would miss the essential point: almost every practice for which prototyping plays a significant role gives the term a unique flavour. While we have been able to find a way to group them together loosely, the presence of so many practices prepared to contribute uniquely to this compendium makes the point far more powerfully than focusing on a smaller set of contributors could ever have done.

Our first act of gratitude is therefore to acknowledge the fifty practices for their generosity, in terms of both spirit and time. Their invaluable contributions have helped us encapsulate the creative zeitgeist that has emerged from the maturation of digital design, prototyping and fabrication processes. To everyone in the following list, our deepest thanks:

Martin Antemann, Blumer-Lehmann
Ben Aranda, Aranda\Lasch
Maximiliano Arrocet, AL_A
Bruce Bell, Facit Homes
Francis Bitonti, Francis Bitonti Studio
Tim Black, BKK Architects
Cristiano Ceccato, Zaha Hadid Architects
Ed Clark, Arup
Alan Dempsey, Nex—
Christian Derix, SUPERSPACE
Anna Dyson, CASE RPI
Jordi Faulí, Sagrada Família
Marc Fornes, TheVeryMany
Bernhard Franken, Franken/Architekten
Jeanne Gang, Studio Gang
Mark Goulthorpe, dECOi architects
Manfred Grohmann, Marc Fahlbusch and
    Kim Boris Löffler, Bollinger + Grohmann
Kasper Guldager Jensen, 3XN
Thomas Heatherwick, Heatherwick Studio
Michael Hensel, OCEAN Design
    Research Association
Mike Holland, Xavier De Kestelier and
    James White, Foster + Partners
Rory Hyde, Victoria and Albert Museum
Eva Jiricna, Eva Jiricna Architects
Christopher Kelly, Architecture Workshop
Asif Khan, Asif Khan Ltd
Bill Kreysler, Kreysler & Associates
Raymond Lau, GAP Architects
Greg Lynn, Greg Lynn Form
Ma Yansong and Dang Qun,
    MAD Architects
Scott Marble, Marble Fairbanks
Achim Menges, ICD
Michael Meredith, MOS Architects
Hugo Mulder, Arup
Kas Oosterhuis, ONL [Oosterhuis_Lénárd]
Jenny B. Osuldsen, Snøhetta
Jonathan Rabagliati, Foster + Partners
Enric Ruiz-Geli, Cloud 9 Architects
Steve Sanderson, CASE Inc.
Fabian Scheurer, designtoproduction
Chris Sharples, SHoP
Bob Sheil, Bartlett School of Architecture
Alvise Simondetti, Arup
Benedetta Tagliabue, EMBT
Martin Tamke, CITA
Michael Taylor, Hopkins Architects
Kerstin Thompson, KTA Architects
Jordi Truco and Sylvia Felipe, HYBRIDa
Michael Trudgeon, Crowd Productions
Nicholas Williams and John Cherrey, SIAL
Philip Yuan, Archi-Union

Secondly, we are extremely grateful to the following individuals at Thames & Hudson: Lucas Dietrich, commissioning editor, not only for his perspicacity in proposing the topic, encouraging a design-process focus, but also for his forbearance during what turned out to be quite a lengthy writing process; Mark Ralph, copy-editor and project manager, who has been both patient and collegially supportive along the way; and Alex Wright, designer, for the remarkable way in which he locked on to the book's message from the outset and steered the graphic design, the font creation and the overall look and form towards the final result.

We would both like to thank RMIT University for providing us with the space and time to move the project forwards. The Australian Research Council generously funded an earlier major research enquiry entitled 'Homo Faber'. Together with colleagues Professor Peter Downton, Professor Andrea Mina and Professor Michael Ostwald, we made an incursion into the extended role of the model in practice. Our discoveries along that particular trajectory guided us towards this prototyping-for-architecture journey. The University of Melbourne is also owed thanks for its contribution of resources during the final stages of the book's preparation.

Lastly, we acknowledge the tireless contribution of our former research associate Andy Miller.

Mark Burry is Professor of Urban Futures in the Faculty of Architecture, Building and Planning at the University of Melbourne. He was previously the founding director of the Design Research Institute (DRI) at RMIT University in Melbourne, and in 2001 was the founder of RMIT's Spatial Information Architecture Laboratory (SIAL). He is a practising architect who has published widely on two main themes: the life, work and theories of Antoni Gaudí, and putting theory into practice with regard to 'challenging' architecture. Since 1979 he has been Senior Architect to the Sagrada Família Basilica Foundation in Spain.

Jane Burry is an architect and Associate Professor of Architecture and Design in the School of Architecture and Design at RMIT University, where she directs the Spatial Information Architecture Laboratory. She has taught, researched and practised internationally, including in Barcelona, where she worked as a project architect in the technical office of Antoni Gaudí's Sagrada Família. She has more than seventy publications to her name, including, as lead author, *The New Mathematics of Architecture* (2010) and, as editor, *Designing the Dynamic* (2013). Her research focuses on mathematics in contemporary design.